Becoming a Fundraiser

The Principles and Practice of Library Development

by

Victoria Steele
Stephen D. Elder

AMERICAN LIBRARY ASSOCIATION

Chicago and London
1992

Cover and text designed by Charles Bozett

Composed by Publishing Services, Inc. in Caslon
on Xyvision/Cg8600

Printed on 55-pound Glatfelter, a pH-neutral stock, and
bound in C1S cover stock by Edwards Brothers

The paper used in this publication meets the minimum
requirements of American National Standard for Information Sciences—Permanence of Paper for Printed Library
Materials, ANSI Z39.48—1984.∞

Library of Congress Cataloging-in-Publication Data

Steele, Victoria.
    Becoming a fundraiser : the principles and practice of
library development / by Victoria Steele and Stephen
D. Elder.
        p.   cm.
    Includes bibliographical references (p.   ) and index.
    ISBN 0-8389-0589-7
    1. Library fund raising.   2. Public libraries—Finance.
I. Elder, Stephen D.   II. Title.   III. Title: Becoming a
fund raiser.
Z683.S74   1992
025.1′1—dc20   92-11940
                                                    CIP

Printed in the United States of America.

96 95 94 93 92   5 4 3 2 1

Contents

Figures

Foreword

Libraries are changing dramatically. The traditional function of libraries as preservers and providers of knowledge and information remains constant, but the packaging of information now involves various computer and telecommunications media that were unknown only a short time ago. Libraries everywhere are faced with the dual challenge of maintaining their traditional resources while incorporating new technologies into their operations and administration.

Partly as a result of these changes, it has become increasingly difficult for libraries to find the support to maintain and improve their collections and services. Where once the budgetary allocations of the university president's office, the city council, or the state legislature sufficed to support the health and growth of libraries, today these funding sources often prove inadequate. If libraries are to sustain current levels of excellence, and if they are to grow to meet the needs of a technologically sophisticated age, they will have to discover new networks of funding.

To secure money from previously untapped sources, librarians must implement innovative and aggressive funding approaches. Fundraising can no longer be an afterthought or a tangential activity labeled a "non-library" function. Raising funds will be imperative to the growth and maintenance of first-rate libraries. In the coming decades fundraising will literally make the difference, for many libraries, between mediocrity and excellence.

The increasing diversity of library services will require library leaders to define and articulate to the communities they serve the mission and priorities of their libraries. If they cannot communicate a clear message about who they are, what they do, and why their health and growth are absolutely essential to the health of the community and the culture of which they are part, libraries will face institutional identity crises, both internally and externally. A fundraising-oriented development program provides a vehicle for explaining the nature and function of the library to the community in order to obtain the support needed to realize the full potential of the library of the future.

Unfortunately, few librarians have been trained in fundraising. Fundraising involves issues and ideas that may be new to them. To make things more difficult, fundraising issues are themselves rather murky and not susceptible, in many cases, to quantitative analysis or clear guidelines.

This book fills a conspicuous void. It tells you how library fundraising works—not how it is supposed to work, but how it truly works. It provides a more comprehensive and realistic view of library development than has previously been available. It tells you what you need to know as a library director, administrator, search committee member, development officer, or simply as a librarian otherwise interested or engaged in fundraising. It explains how to think about library fundraising. Above all, it tells you how to succeed.

After you read this book, you should know enough to decide what kind of a fundraising program is right for you. You will not fail in your declared fundraising goals because you will have selected a program that *will* be successful. You will have learned that a key element in successful fundraising is choosing a program that suits your administrative and personal capacities, inclinations, and talents. This book will enable you to choose between a modest or a high-powered program, as your own circumstances suggest. You will not make the mistake of announcing a multimillion-dollar library campaign and having it fall spectacularly flat. And, if you do elect to announce publicly a multimillion-dollar campaign, you will be able do so with confidence because you will know that you have the elements in place to be successful.

Development involves, on one level, communicating the value of an organization to society. Some librarians may feel that, in comparison to other organizations, theirs are comparatively lacking in general appeal. This is not so. Many people in our society are painfully aware that they are living in a cultural vacuum, in a climate dominated by commercial vulgarity. Like the arts, libraries are compelling to many people. Libraries offer the pleasures of intellectual enrichment and learning. There are people who are starved for the experiences libraries can offer. As librarians move into the development field, it is important that they look at their organizations not only as repositories of information but also as centers of learning and cultural activity.

Fundraising offers an opportunity to ennoble and expand one's vision and to break out of ordinary patterns. It offers the chance to link our bold ideas and exciting plans with a donor's ambition and ability to realize them.

Fundraising requires intellectual agility on many levels. It requires the ability to assess creatively an organization's strengths and to build on them, to formulate a mission, to articulate a vision, and to relate all of this to internal and external constituencies.

Ultimately, this book is not only about library development; it is also about library leadership.

SUSAN K. NUTTER
Director of Libraries
North Carolina State University

Preface

Twenty years ago, after interviewing librarians, development officers, and grant makers throughout the country, Andrew Eaton made a number of astute observations about librarians and fundraising: [1]

> Fundraising has been a relatively neglected aspect of university librarianship. Very little has been written about it, and most librarians have, for various reasons, considered it none of their business. . . . Some librarians may hesitate to become fund raisers on the ground that they are not suited for the job by personality or temperament. If they had been cut out to be salesmen, they may argue, they would not have chosen librarianship as a career. . . . It is probably fair to say that the typical university librarian's attitude toward fund raising is that this is a responsibility which primarily belongs to others. [2]

In the two decades since his article, the situation Eaton described has not much changed. An increasing number of librarians have turned to fundraising, some because of desperation, some because they were required to, and some because it seemed to be a means by which to realize a vision. But few librarians have been prepared, either by training or by temperament, to undertake an ambitious development program. Those librarians who have pursued fundraising have not had a published body of theory nor much in the way of practical technique to guide them. As in any budding field, the literature and support organizations available to them have failed to keep pace with their needs and have done little to address their uneasiness with fundraising. The literature has been unfocused, undeveloped in its thinking and approaches, and sometimes just plain wrong. Moreover, conferences and workshops on fundraising rarely focus on the unique needs of libraries and the librarians guiding them. [3]

   This book is intended as a kind of *vade mecum* for librarians engaged in, or embarking on, fundraising. Like its antecedents, this guide is meant to alert travelers to dangers and to direct them toward safe havens. It advises, "Take this direction; beware of that one."

We first became aware that the way needed showing when, as new library fundraisers, we sought guidance. We read the available literature, investigated professional associations, participated in classes and workshops, and asked questions of other fundraisers. Although this process gave us useful information, it became apparent that much of the way simply had not been charted and that we would have to discover it for ourselves.

There are only a handful of books on library development. Most of these are compilations of papers written by a host of people from different backgrounds that describe selected features of the landscape, and, unfortunately, they are almost always the *same* features, and not the ones we consider to be "the Alps," the important obstacles to be surmounted. The monographic literature in the development field is no more illuminating and is aimed at professional fundraisers rather than librarians. This is especially true of the oft-mentioned *Designs for Fund Raising* by Harold Seymour. Another frequently recommended book, Jerold Panas's *Mega Gifts,* primarily concerns donor motivation; though inspiring, it is more analogous to reading the lives of the saints than finding your way to the Holy Land. It tells the stories of noted philanthropists but does not indicate how to gain philanthropic support for your own institution.

The one important exception to this dearth of useful books on development is Kathleen Kelly's recent, ground-breaking book, *Fund Raising and Public Relations: A Critical Analysis.*[4] Kelly's book is the first to attempt to provide a theoretical context for fundraising based on a critical analysis of the field and the way it functions. Her impressive effort to forge the beginnings of a substantive theory to guide fundraising, along with her suggestions for future research, are major contributions. But, as she herself argues, the current fundraising literature is incomplete, misleading, and lacking in explanatory power; based on flawed assumptions; and the result of misconceptions and myths.[5] And her own book, as valuable as it is in illuminating the misconceptions and myths, is not concerned with library development.

Insofar as the periodical literature is concerned, it is indicative of the state of the art that "fund raising" is not a searchable term in *Library Literature.* While there is a good deal of information about grants, we could find nothing that helped a beginner step-by-step through the process of soliciting a major gift. By the same token, we found many surveys that quantified the fact that librarians were *doing* fundraising but no real information about *how* they were doing it. And though we discovered some articles describing particular attempts to raise small amounts of money by means of book sales, car washes, bake sales, and so on, we could not find guidance on more ambitious efforts. To be sure, there are a few articles that contain useful nuggets of information, but these nuggets are often embedded in misinformation.

Ultimately, the literature we found most useful was in the fields of management and communications. In particular, in the areas of planning, problem solving, and leadership, we came to value Gerald Nadler and Shozo Hibino's *Breakthrough Thinking* and Harold Leavitt's *Corporate Pathfinders*. In formulating a methodology for soliciting major gifts that is open and ethical, we profited from Robert Miller and Stephen Heiman's *Conceptual Selling*. For their work on effectiveness through self-knowledge, we are grateful to Warren Bennis, Burt Nanus, Katharine Briggs, and Isabel Briggs Myers. We also value Robert Cialdini's work on personal influence and the larger body of work on communication theory.

We also investigated the professional organizations in the fundraising field. Though there is no support system for fundraisers equivalent to that found in the library field, there are two professional organizations for fundraisers: the National Society of Fundraising Executives (NSFRE) and the Council for Advancement and Support of Education (CASE). The former encompasses fundraisers from all areas, including those in health, welfare, and religion. CASE serves a variety of advancement professionals in higher education, including public relations, admissions, and publications officers as well as development staff. These organizations primarily provide networking opportunities for their members. CASE publishes a journal called *Currents,* but since membership in CASE is institutional rather than individual not many fundraisers see it regularly, so it does not provide a professional organ comparable to, say, *American Libraries.*

In 1987, a small group of development officers working in academic libraries organized themselves into a nonaffiliated group called DORAL, Development Officers of Research Academic Libraries. This group is a positive approach to advancing the field, and its formation indicates the need library development professionals have for a forum that enables them to share information among themselves. Its meetings, which are not open to library leaders, allow members to discuss freely how to help library administrators better understand fundraising. In order to keep its size manageable, DORAL capped its membership shortly after its formation.

Both NSFRE and CASE offer training seminars. The Fund Raising and Financial Development Section (FRFDS) of the Library Administration and Management Association (LAMA) of the American Library Association has offered for the last several years preconference workshops on fundraising, too. There is some valuable basic information to be gleaned from some of these classes, but there is some misinformation, too. We offer this caution: beware of trying to apply to libraries the approaches presented by seminar leaders who draw primarily from nonlibrary models.

There are significant differences between raising money for libraries, especially academic libraries, and raising money for other types of organizations. The critical difference between fundraising for an academic library and fundraising for the symphony or a theatrical company is this: the former depends on the leadership of the library director, whereas the latter depends primarily on organizing volunteer leadership from the community. Apart from religious fundraising, most of the fundraising that goes on in this country involves the second type of leadership. From hospitals to the United Way, the key to raising money is to enlist the involvement of the wealthiest, most influential people in the community. Without volunteer leadership, these organizations simply could not raise significant amounts of money.

In libraries, however, volunteer leadership is not nearly as critical as library leadership. If the library is seeking funds in support of bold and exciting plans, donors want and expect to hear about it from the library's CEO, that is, the library director. A successful library development program requires the active involvement of librarians themselves. A development officer can provide guidance, ideas, and energy, but the nature of fundraising makes it essential that the library director be the central figure in the effort. By virtue of the director's position and the prestige that accrues to it, the director is frequently the only person who "counts" to donors.

A few words about our own experience in this field may be useful. One of us comes from a communications background and was, during the writing of this book, a development officer for the University of Southern California (USC) Libraries. He is currently a Senior Development Officer for the University of Redlands. The other is currently the head of Special Collections at USC. She was previously the Director of Development for the Libraries and the Graduate School of Library and Information Science at the University of California, Los Angeles (UCLA) and headed two special collections at UCLA before taking that post. For years, the two of us have been interested in discovering what makes a library development program successful.

Because we both come from academic library backgrounds, we have drawn many of our examples from the academic environment we know best. However, this book is written with all librarians in mind, and we hope it will be useful to our colleagues in public libraries and independent research libraries.

Given the needs of our audience, and given our own experience, we wanted to write a practical book. Since we did not, however, want to descend to mere impressionism, as so many other books do, we have endeavored to avail ourselves of such theory as exists, presently codified by Kathleen Kelly.

A few words about the style of this book may also be appropriate. Clear and engaging communication was our objective. In trying to achieve this goal, we emulated the most recent literature of the management and communications fields. This literature, unlike much of the writing in the library field, uses the active voice and the second person, and employs straightforward language. The use of masculine pronouns in some instances, and feminine in others, was strictly an editorial decision and is not meant to imply exclusiveness of gender.

Having learned all we could from the existing literature, professional organizations, and workshops, we set out on the fundraising road ourselves. We found that parts of the road had been described from hearsay and tradition rather than direct experience. Other parts had not been described at all. This book is the result of our journey; we hope it will make your journey easier.

We are interested in hearing from readers, both librarians and fundraisers, about your experiences with library development and your responses to this book. Write to us care of:

> American Library Association
> Books
> 50 East Huron Street
> Chicago, IL 60611

NOTES

1. Throughout this book we spell "fundraising" and "fundraiser" as one word. Many dictionaries hyphenate the spellings or give them as two separate words. Some dictionaries distinguish nominative use (not hyphenated) from adjectival use (hyphenated). We advocate the spelling of fundraising and fundraiser as one word in the interests of simplicity and on-line retrievability.

2. Andrew Eaton, "Fund Raising for University Libraries," *College and Research Libraries* 32 (Sept. 1971): 351–353.

3. Libraries have been so little involved in fundraising that, in the university setting, the library, in comparison with all other areas, comes in dead last in terms of support. See Council for Aid to Education, *Voluntary Support of Education 1990–91*, 2 vols. (New York: Council for Aid to Education, 1991), vol. 1: *National Estimates and Survey Summary*, p. 14.

4. Kathleen S. Kelly, *Fund Raising and Public Relations: A Critical Analysis* (Hillsdale, N.J.: Lawrence Erlbaum, 1991).

5. Ibid., pp. 2–3.

Acknowledgments

We have benefited from the support and encouragement of many friends. Special thanks go to John V. Richardson, Jr., for believing in the project from the beginning and for his invaluable advice along the way. We are indebted to several generous colleagues and friends who read the manuscript and offered intelligent and helpful feedback: Dorothy Anderson, Larry E. Burgess, Kathy E. S. Donahue, Olive C. R. James, Joan Kunselman, Susan K. Nutter, Mary Jane Perna, and Susan Rice. We are especially grateful to our spouses, Jane Elder and Tim Steele, for their patience and forbearance while we saw this project to completion. To Tim we are especially grateful for his close reading of the manuscript and for his understanding and inspiration. And, to each other, we owe the rest.

Introduction

Charitable organizations face a double-edged sword: In order to enhance their autonomy, they must seek external funding to support their institutional goals, but in so doing, they risk losing autonomy by accepting gifts that limit their power to determine goals and the means of pursuing those goals.

KATHLEEN KELLY
*Fund Raising and Public Relations:
A Critical Analysis*

This introduction provides a chapter-by-chapter overview of this book. Before proceeding to the summary, however, we wish to enunciate the principles and tenets that underlie the fundraising approach we describe. We believe these principles and tenets have general validity and may be useful touchstones for our readers as they try to evaluate other approaches to fundraising.[1]

The principles are:

1. Library fundraising seeks consonance between a donor's wishes and a library's needs. Hence, it should proceed in an open, ethical, balanced, win-win way.
2. Fundraising is judged to be successful when it results in gifts that contribute to the strategic vision for the library; gifts should free a library to achieve its goals rather than hamper or distract it from its mission.

In addition to our two principles, we hold four fundraising tenets:

1. Successful fundraising depends on the leadership and participation of the library director.
2. Development is more effective when it avoids a formulaic approach and instead recognizes that every library setting, library staff, group of potential donors, and set of circumstances is unique.

1

3. Development is more effective when it discards a widespread fundraising fallacy: that successful fundraising rests on and requires a broad base of donors. Statistics show that as much as 90 percent of all giving is done by only 10 percent of all donors.[2]
4. Development is more effective when it rejects traditional marketing and sales approaches and associated vocabulary. Since both approaches are one-sided (sales approaches "push" products on customers and marketing approaches adjust or mold products in response to consumers), they violate the two-way, balanced approach postulated in the first principle.

If this book has a leitmotif, it is that leadership and self-knowledge are essential to successful development. This book is written for library directors who are also leaders. As they take their organizations into unmapped territories, leaders must be confident and persuasive. It is with them in mind that Chapter 1 begins with the fundamental question, "How compatible am I with the activities of fundraising?" This question is not often addressed in the development literature, perhaps because it is so sensitive and personal, and perhaps because of the false assumption that anyone can be a successful fundraiser. Before looking outward—to feasibility studies and plans, for instance—everyone new to fundraising should look inward. More and more, fundraising will make the difference between mediocre libraries and excellent ones. In Chapter 1, we try to help library directors come to a realistic assessment of their own abilities and talents for fundraising.

Chapter 1 examines librarians' attitudes and fears about raising money and openly confronts their personal barriers. It also addresses the most essential ingredient in successful fundraising: leadership ability. Fundraising requires visionary leadership; a librarian undertaking major-gifts fundraising must be willing to take risks in an entrepreneurial way. Major donors are not interested in talking to fundraisers; they want to talk to the library's CEO. *Money wants to talk to power.* Professional fundraisers—development officers—are like Sherpa guides: they get the leaders to the tops of the mountains by leading the way and by carrying the bulk of the luggage. But library leaders must climb the mountains with them—fundraising cannot be delegated. Avoiding or neglecting a fundraising effort, once launched, creates what we call a *latch-key* development program. It is also essential that library leaders keep before them one or two clear and realistic development priorities. Vacillation about priorities from a long menu of needs is deadly to a development program.

At the end of Chapter 1, we outline three test areas that can indicate your potential to be an effective fundraiser. We also say a few words about developing a program that fits your personal style.

Chapter 2 introduces basic concepts, divided for ease of discussion into two camps: (1) "The Science of Fundraising," or those concepts which reveal common terms, regular patterns, and predictable cycles, and (2) "The Art of Fundraising," or those concepts that are more complex, highly situational, and rely on good instincts and an understanding of donor psychology. In the science of fundraising section, library development is defined and described as *a carefully orchestrated, purposive effort to raise substantial sums of money by identifying and cultivating potential donors and by soliciting gifts from them when their goals and wishes are congruent with the library's goals and priorities. Successful fundraising depends on the leadership and participation of the library director. The goal of the development program is to enhance the library's independence. Therefore, fundraising is judged to be effective not principally on the basis of dollars raised, but to the extent that gifts contribute to the strategic vision for the library.*

The science of fundraising involves other important terms and concepts. For example, *prospects* are potential donors who move through a five-step *development cycle:* identification, cultivation (i.e., orchestrated involvement), solicitation, stewardship (the nurturing of a relationship after a gift has been made), and resolicitation. The development cycle takes time, typically thirteen or more contacts over a period of two to three years. To be a viable prospect, a person must have certain characteristics we have formulated into the mnemonic *MAGIC.* Use MAGIC to remind yourself to ask about every prospect: if the person has *means;* what the person's *age* is and if there are heirs; if the person is a *giver;* if the person is *involved* in your organization; and if the person has *contacts,* that is, the ability to give away other people's money. We point out that the vast majority of major gifts will come from a relatively small number of prospects, most of whom will already be known to you. We urge you to avoid "vague others" and "busybodies."

Chapter 2 also introduces the important distinction between *annual giving* (a fundraising method that produces large numbers of small gifts) and *major giving* (a method that produces a small number of large gifts). It emphasizes the need to understand this basic concept so that you and your fundraiser spend your time appropriately, depending on the type of program you have decided is right for you. The distinction is also fundamental to the methods you employ when asking for a gift. Annual-giving programs use mass communication methods, namely mail and telephone. Major gifts require a face-to-face, personalized approach.

Chapter 2 also describes the role of a support group in a development program using the analogy of the fundraising swimming pool. In addition, it addresses the questions: Who will give to my library? How do I ask them? To what will people give? How do I thank them?

In Chapter 2, the Art of Fundraising section discusses the ways donors give to satisfy their own needs, not the library's needs. Donors respond to big ideas, not to projects that seem operational (e.g., retrospective conversion) or that appear to be huge and insurmountable (e.g., preserving the general collections of the library). Many donors want their names on rooms and other spaces in your library, and they expect to be accorded special privileges. Donors also give when they believe in an organization's mission and in its leader. Lastly, the art of fundraising involves donor strategy, a subject we discuss by drawing on research in communication theory.

Chapter 3 guides the library director in building and working with a development team. First, we discuss how to choose staffing levels and configurations that fit your program and goals. Second, we describe how to select and work with development professionals. The next section is devoted specifically to development staffing for academic libraries, including what advantages may be gained from working cooperatively with the central development office of universities. Then, relying on the metaphor of the mountain climber and Sherpa guide, we discuss the role of librarians in the library development team. Finally, we return to the fundraising swimming pool metaphor to illustrate how the team works together to coordinate the development process.

Creating your program through an understanding of your library's purposes and uniqueness is the subject of Chapter 4. Your organization's uniqueness interacts with its purposes, creating a niche that is yours alone. An understanding of your niche helps you to characterize yourself effectively to others (a key activity in fundraising) and helps you in making decisions to accept money and collections that dovetail well with your niche. Since your niche is unique, it follows that your development program will be as well. The programs of other libraries will not necessarily fit your niche, so do not try to emulate them; instead, create your own.

Chapter 4 also examines the issue of development plans. For development purposes, the most important plans are the strategic plans of the library and its parent institution. All-purpose case statements and most development plans are too general, formulaic, and untimely to be effective. We prefer instead project-specific proposals that take into account the unique factors at work in every development situation. This approach helps you avoid formula fundraising.

Chapter 4 concludes by addressing the important topic of evaluating your fundraising program. Rather than adopting the simplistic approach of measuring per annum dollars raised, we recommend that you instead: (1) evaluate fundraising based on total dollars *and* gift utility; (2) adopt an evaluation time frame longer than one year; and (3) evaluate the *process* of fundraising in addition to the *outcome*. To evaluate programs in this way is to recognize that fundraising is effective not when it reaps ever-increasing dollar amounts, but when gifts support the library's goals and when the fundraising effort communicates with donors and other key constituencies in a way that preserves the library's independence.

In Chapter 5 we walk you through the process of soliciting a major gift. We advocate an approach that is ethical, open in its intentions, and conducive to a win-win outcome. Based on new research about how people make decisions, we update outmoded sales concepts that have been applied to fundraising. The chapter covers real-life situations, such as how to get an appointment with a major-gift prospect, how to earn credibility, and how to check your timing. It describes the three elements of a development call: getting information, giving information, and getting commitment. Careful questioning is the essence of these encounters, for it helps you to identify those prospects you should pursue and those you should not pursue. Your questioning of prospects keeps the focus where it should be. It also allows you to uncover your prospects' mind-sets, their preconceived ideas about your library, your institution, and possibly your cause based on their past experiences. We give you guidance on determining when it is time to ask someone for a gift, what to say when you ask, and how to use silences strategically.

In Chapter 6 we move to the topic of library Friends groups. In order to support a fundraising program, a Friends group must be managed with the development purpose clearly in the forefront. Goodwill and the minimal income produced from dues (an amount easily surpassed by one major gift) are not enough to justify a Friends group from a development perspective. To serve a development purpose, a Friends group should: (1) raise endowment; (2) be assigned to development staff and be run by the library, rather than volunteers; (3) host fun activities; (4) recruit members on the basis of MAGIC; (5) see the library director as the focal point; and (6) form one part of the library's annual-giving base. Friends groups should *not*: (1) form an exclusive club; (2) have as their main activity buying books for the library; (3) be assigned to a librarian with other responsibilities or be left to run themselves; (4) host unimaginative events, especially ones that focus on esoteric subjects or library operations; (5) build membership the populist way (bigger = better); (6) see the library director as playing a minor role; and (7) comprise the only annual-giving activity. The final part of the chapter is a collection of answers to commonly asked questions about Friends groups; membership levels and benefits, billing, and publications are all covered, along with trickier issues such as support groups for branch libraries and the problem of Friends groups that are narrowly focused on special collections.

Special events are the subject of Chapter 7. Group gatherings in general have some important drawbacks that limit their fundraising power. Practically speaking, most events are not generators of income, they are expenders of it. Additionally, the personal interaction possible in the context of an event allows relationships to progress only to a limited point; in development, more intimate contacts are necessary to progress in a relationship with a prospect. Though events are an important development tool, they are not where the bulk of fundraising takes place, contrary to what many people believe.

Chapter 7 looks at development events from the point of view of the library director, focusing on the following five key ideas for getting the most mileage out of events. As a library director, you need to: (1) understand the relationship of events to development; (2) understand the four types of library events—Friends events, cultivation events, recognition events, and fundraising events—and their purposes; (3) pay as much attention to the feelings that will be evoked by an event as to the actual content; (4) understand your role in setting the tone, style, and image for the library; and (5) master the art of effectiveness in group situations. As a library director, be concerned with how you come across in group situations, realizing that people will read you in quasi-symbolic terms. Develop the skills that allow you to accomplish development goals in group settings, an art we introduce in this chapter.

The final section of Chapter 7 deals with the anatomy of a fundraiser, specifically the Friends of the USC Libraries' Scripter Award. This case study is instructive in three specific ways: (1) it illustrates how a fundraising event can be used to serve a number of development purposes beyond the bounds of the occasion itself, (2) it demonstrates how an idea can be used to connect the library to a glamorous and monied segment of the community, and (3) it provides specific details about how to package and orchestrate an event. It also candidly spells out the drawbacks inherent in such an event.

Chapter 8 addresses the subject of raising money from corporations, foundations, and planned-giving prospects. If you have access to specialists in these areas in your organization, your first priority should be to cultivate close relationships with them; they have both contacts and the ability to direct gifts your way if they are inclined to do so. It is essential to understand that gifts from foundations and corporations rarely come about as the result of an impersonal application process. In fact, they come from individuals in those organizations, and these individuals should be identified and cultivated just as you would any other individual major-gift prospect. In the section on planned giving, we deal with practical problems associated with planned-giving calls, such as how to handle the subject of death and how to find out a prospect's age and assets. Using a tree-and-fruit analogy, the chapter provides an easy method for explaining two of the most common planned-giving instruments—charitable remainder trusts and charitable lead trusts. The chapter concludes with a guide to understanding and explaining the benefits of planned gifts and covers how much to emphasize them.

Chapter 9 offers ways that you can enhance your library's image by communicating strategically with your library's constituencies. Using the right tool (communication instrument) for the right job (communicating the right messages to the right constituency) allows you to go beyond the vague notions of "raising visibility" and "getting publicity." The crucial differences between public relations and development serve to introduce the basics of managing your communications strategically. Another example shows how these techniques might be used in a fairly sophisticated way to improve the image of the library. In a section devoted to outreach materials, we devote particular attention to development publications. The chapter concludes with an examination of image, providing both an image self-test and guidance on conducting an image audit.

The concluding chapter looks to the future. We observe that in the rapidly developing technological environment, librarians have begun to shift their focus from the internal functions of libraries to external technologies, markets, and opportunities—a positive orientation for library development. An outward focus and an openness to change and to nontraditional approaches are complementary to fundraising. We have begun to connect, to seek new kinds of relationships, to forge partnerships, to be entrepreneurial. These changes help librarians create an environment that is alive with opportunity.

How will changes in the very function of the library affect the library fundraising climate of the future? We speculate that keeping things personal and tangible in an increasingly electronic environment may be the overarching challenge of library development in the future. We conclude that if, as librarians, we can become adept fundraisers, we can ensure the future excellence of libraries.

NOTES

1. These principles and tenets infuse our book. In arriving at several of them, we are indebted to Kathleen S. Kelly for her seminal study, *Fund Raising and Public Relations: A Critical Analysis* (Hillsdale, N.J.: Lawrence Erlbaum, 1991).

2. Ibid., pp. 278–279.

CHAPTER 1

Fundraising and You

A Personal Feasibility Study

You often hear from development consultants and experienced fundraisers that the first thing you need to do before launching a fundraising campaign is to undertake a feasibility study. But feasibility studies look outward. Before looking outward, everyone new to fundraising first should look inward. Librarians contemplating a development program should examine their own attitudes toward fundraising and ask themselves, "How compatible am I with the activities of fundraising?"

Just as a successful management style results from serious thought about values and goals, so your successful leadership of a fundraising initiative derives from a focused, informed assessment of your attitudes about fundraising, your capacities as a leader, and your personal strengths and inclinations. It is essential that librarians go into fundraising with forward-looking and positive goals rather than merely in reaction to problems or out of a desire to emulate other organizations that have gotten into the development act. Though the aim of development is to provide support for libraries, it cannot function as a deficit-closing mechanism or a remedy for budgetary shortfalls. People who give major gifts to libraries do so for substantial and lasting projects rather than temporary expedients. Donors do not give to needs; they give to opportunities. Whether your development program is aimed toward a multimillion-dollar campaign or has more modest objectives, it must proceed in an inspiring, forward-looking way. You must position it as a means for creating resources and facilities for the future, not as a bandage to patch up old injuries.

Each successful library leader must set his or her own tone, direction, and style. Different libraries have different needs and characters; they serve different communities and constituencies. What works in one case may not work in another. Development is a field in which the personalities of the librarian and the prospective donors play crucial roles. There are no hard-and-fast rules for many aspects of fundraising. Unless librarians examine their basic assumptions about fundraising, and unless they are sensitive to the different ways of tailoring development efforts to their institutions and their personalities, they will not create an effective program.

If you stop to think about it, you probably have a variety of attitudes about fundraising. You might believe, for example, that fundraising is a form of organized begging and the very thought of asking for money is distasteful to you. You might think, as one librarian once remarked, "My mother didn't raise me to ask people for money." You might feel, as another librarian did, that "Rich people intimidate me." You might be so used to organizational hierarchy that the idea of asking someone outside your organization to help you seems inappropriate. Or, having heard fundraisers speak of "cultivating prospects" and of "solicitations," you may feel that the very vocabulary of development suggests a kind of institutional prostitution.

It is not necessary to root out these attitudes from your basic beliefs. They are perfectly natural. As librarians, we appreciate the intrinsic value of our organizations; it sometimes distresses us that others do not appreciate them as readily. Many of us are dismayed by the emphasis our society places on material wealth; we have anxieties about dealing with money and feel uneasy around those who have a great deal of it. Trained to be intellectually scrupulous, librarians may be repelled by the hype and hustle that they suspect development entails.

Since psychological anxieties and personal barriers are difficult to discuss, most books about fundraising ignore them altogether and dwell exclusively on the supposed "nuts and bolts" of the subject, suggesting, tacitly, that there really is nothing to fundraising but following a few formulas. This is a mistake. If you do not know how to think about fundraising and about yourself in relation to it, you can make many false starts and wrong choices about the nuts and bolts and become frustrated and discouraged.

FEARS

Almost everyone new to fundraising is initially fearful of it. It is only natural to be uneasy about an enterprise in which you have little or no experience, especially if it is as foreign as fundraising probably is to you if you are a librarian. This unease might be caused by any mixture of four fears that librarians face when contemplating development: (1) the fear of failing at raising money, (2) the fear of being turned down when asking for money, (3) the fear of not being accepted socially by the monied donors with whom they will be in contact, and (4) the fear of "prostituting" themselves.

The first fear involves that sinking feeling that "some of my peers seem to be able to raise money, but can I?" You might tell yourself that if you have the ability to manage a staff and a budget you should be able to raise money. But what if, as you may correctly surmise, many of the skills required for this work are completely different from those that have contributed to your success as a librarian?

It would be easiest to say, "Everyone can successfully raise money!" Unfortunately, however, not everyone can. This chapter contains specific techniques for coming to an honest and realistic assessment of your potential as a fundraiser. For now, remember this: your *desire* to succeed as a fundraiser is essential. Telling yourself "I can do it" is a good start. If you have a strong desire to raise funds, it will be easier to overcome attitudinal blocks, give up some things you like to do in order to devote time to it, and find the nerve to venture out into unknown territory.

How can you overcome the second fear, the fear of being turned down by a donor? One thing to do is to remember that the "you" that is involved in soliciting funds is the "institutional you"—not the "personal you." You are acting in a professional capacity as an official representative of your institution. It might also help to keep the situation in perspective by bearing in mind that asking someone for money is far less risky emotionally than many other things we do in our lives—interviewing for jobs or forming personal relationships, for example. Another way to deal with the fear of being turned down is to remember that everyone involved in fundraising gets turned down frequently—even the most skilled fundraisers. It is disappointing to be turned down after months, even years, of effort have gone into a solicitation. But in fundraising, as in baseball, batting 3 out of 10 is good. When you are turned down, at least you have received an answer and you can go on to focus on other possibilities without harboring further false hopes. When you are successful the experience is exhilarating, and it will more than compensate for the disappointments.

Many librarians also fear that they will not be socially accepted by their donors. As they embark on a fundraising program, they wonder if they should be reading up on wine and reviewing their French. They might guess, quite correctly, that there are degrees of acceptance into the exclusive social circle, from warm and full admission to chilly exclusion. They wonder where they will end up. This fear is more easily overcome than the previous two because a large majority of library directors have two strong assets going for them. First, as librarians, they are intellectually sophisticated and lively. Second, they have the prestige of their positions behind them, and the power of position has a big impact on donors. These two assets will readily assure them a reasonable level of social acceptance and will prove greatly beneficial to their fundraising efforts in general.

Finally there is the fear of prostituting yourself, of doing something unbecoming or even sleazy. One way to overcome this fear is to recall our two principles of library fundraising:

1. Library fundraising seeks consonance between a donor's wishes and a library's needs. Hence, it should proceed in an open, ethical, balanced, win-win way.
2. Fundraising is judged to be successful when it results in gifts that contribute to the strategic vision for the library; gifts should free a library to achieve its goals rather than hamper or distract it from its mission.

Fundraising conducted according to these two principles eliminates any possible taint and allows you to proceed confidently, secure in the knowledge that what you are doing is both ethical and responsible. This frees you to serve a cause that you know is worthy and that you believe in, and it allows you to communicate your vision with enthusiasm. Your confidence and belief in your cause are, incidentally, more important than personal charm. Potential donors often distrust a glad-handing, superficial approach. They will respond, however, to a sincere, committed approach.

Sometimes when a person has been in a job a long time, it becomes difficult to summon the belief, or at least the energy, necessary to communicate effectively. It is important to ask yourself whether you feel challenged and excited by your library. As the library director, you must supply the intellectual and emotional energy to drive the fundraising program.

VALUE CONFLICTS

Just as you must examine your attitudes and fears about fundraising before launching a development program, so you must be aware of ways in which your political views may affect your relationship with donors. For example, many librarians find themselves politically on the left, while many donor prospects are on the right of the political spectrum. How are you going to deal with comments from donor prospects that are in conflict with your own beliefs? You may be accustomed to an environment that is comprised of different racial, ethnic, and religious groups, and that is open-minded about sexual preferences. Many of America's boardrooms, unfortunately, are not so diverse, nor are they so tolerant of diversity.

If you are, say, a New Deal Democrat and you find yourself in a situation with a prospective donor who complains that Franklin Roosevelt ruined the country, it is not a wise policy to argue with him, as much as you may believe him to be misguided. This does not mean that you need to parrot his beliefs or become a hypocritical toady. Instead, try to maintain a tactful neutrality and look for the earliest opening to change the subject, or use active listening techniques. The object is not to determine how you and the donor differ but how you can establish areas of common ground. Realize that when you are interacting with prospective donors you need not feel overly involved personally; rather, you should regard yourself chiefly as a representative or an embodiment of your institution. In this way, you are a bit like an actor playing a role. This role is in no way duplicitous, but it *is* a role, and, because it may be an awkward one for many librarians, we devote later chapters to providing explicit guidance on handling these interactions.

Another situation that sometimes proves an unnecessary stumbling block if you have not thought about it ahead of time is measuring the library's cause against another in which you, personally, believe strongly. For example, in your heart, you might not believe that your library is as important as helping the homeless or eradicating illiteracy. You might not even realize you feel this way until the day a well-heeled executive wants to give you a huge amount of money to buy books on an esoteric subject for the sole purpose of seeing his or her name on a wall. Suddenly you may experience a crisis of conscience. In these situations, remember that how we feel about such matters is relevant only to us. It is not our business to worry about how others assess their own giving priorities. Donors will give to some causes and not to others; money that does not go to the library will not necessarily go to some other worthy cause. We must not let our personal estimate of the comparative importance of other causes invalidate the library's cause.

LEADERSHIP

Leaders do the right thing. Managers do things right.

WARREN BENNIS

Once you have assessed and come to terms with your attitudes about fundraising, consider your capacities as a leader. Leadership is the most important determinant of fundraising success.

There are two kinds of leadership associated with fundraising: leadership from within an organization and leadership from outside an organization. This chapter addresses the first kind of leadership—the most critical kind to library fundraising. We will have more to say about the second kind, outside (or volunteer) leadership, in chapters 3, 5, and 6.

When we refer to leadership within an organization in connection with fundraising, we refer to the library director's vision, purpose, and sense of mission for the library. A clear vision, purpose, and sense of mission are intrinsic to strong leadership, and they motivate donors; your vision is what you have to offer them.

Harold J. Leavitt of the Graduate School of Business at Stanford University has developed a management model useful for thinking about leadership, development, and libraries.[1] Its purpose is to describe the way people function in organizations. Leavitt's management model can be pictured this way:

1 Pathfinding <—> 2 Problem Solving <—> 3 Implementing

As Leavitt says, pathfinding is about "mission, purpose, and vision." Problem solving is about "analysis, planning, and reasoning"; and implementing is about "doing, changing, and influencing." Every organization depends on a mix of the three modes. The boundaries between the different modes are not hard-and-fast. Nevertheless, this paradigm provides a useful conceptual tool for examining libraries.

Implementing is seen throughout libraries in the work of catalogers, reference librarians, systems librarians, circulation managers, and many others. These are the people who make libraries function on a daily basis. They are good at careful, item-level tasks, at quantifying and organizing material.

Problem solving can be seen in many supervisory positions in libraries. Problem solving requires analysis; analyzing problems and finding solutions are the province of many associate directors, unit heads, department heads, and division heads.[2] These people concern themselves with budgets, personnel policies, systems development, and the like. Most people in problem-solving positions begin their careers as implementers.

Pathfinding is leading. It is visionary, entrepreneurial, and creative. It is sometimes unconventional. It takes into account faith as well as evidence, often even going so far as to violate problem-solving precepts. It is concerned with the big picture. In libraries, pathfinders are sometimes the people who concern themselves more with obtaining collections than with where the books will be stored or how they will be cataloged. They are the people who envision pioneering services, who can see, before there is money to realize the vision, libraries full of people using computers to do new things. They are people who can paint a picture of the future, and they are truly rare birds in all organizations.

Since fundraising requires "pathfinding thinking" and vision, a librarian interested in major-gifts fundraising must be a pathfinder. Without strong leadership, high-stakes fundraising goes nowhere.

Pathfinding Leadership in Libraries

Many studies have established a direct correlation between a university president's willingness and capacity for leadership of the development effort and the success of the fundraising program.[3] A parallel situation exists in the library. Just as the president of a college or university is the central figure in a successful development program—the institution's chief fundraiser—so the library director is the key figure in the library's fundraising program. The leadership and status of the library director are critical. The director is the CEO and brings the backing and confidence of the organization that determined that he or she was the best person for the job.

Usually, a major donor will feel that it is not appropriate for him to interact with anyone lower organizationally than the director. *Money wants to talk to power.* Generally, potential donors are not interested in talking to subordinates or to a development officer, if there is one. Development officers and other subordinates who assist the director with fund-raising act as Sherpa guides. Just as a guide's job is to get his charges to the top of the mountain, so a development officer's success lies in helping the library director meet, get to know, and effectively solicit major-donor prospects. The library director and the donors get the glory; the Sherpa guide's satisfaction comes from knowing that the mountain climbers could not have reached the peak without him. Development officers make sure that all the necessary tasks get done (e.g., follow-up letters, proposals, and thank you letters), but it is the library director's vision that is the reason for the expedition in the first place.

Fundraising cannot be delegated. You cannot ask others to climb the mountain for you; *there is no reason for them to climb it unless you are climbing it, too.* It follows, then, that you can have a fundraising program without a development officer but not without a library director. Fundraising programs can be sustained with vacant development positions, but they are nearly impossible to sustain without leadership from the library director. A sure sign that a library director does not understand this fundamental truth may be found in this all-too-common scenario: A library director, like many of his colleagues, devotes a large portion of his time to professional conferences. After long absences, he returns and asks his development staff, "So, how is the fundraising going?" The likely response, given the necessity of the director's participation in the fundraising process, will be, "Not very well." Be careful not to create, through avoidance and neglect, what we call a *latch-key* development program.

Two Implications of Pathfinding for Library Fundraising

1. *You can't do it all.* Fundraising offers the library director the challenge of being the visionary, of letting someone else count the beans. It no longer matters that she knows everything about the daily operation of her library. Pathfinders do not pride themselves on their mastery of detail, an "implementing" activity; if anything, mastery of detail and pathfinding are antithetical. University presidents spend three quarters of their time raising money. Similarly, if the library director wants to raise substantial sums of money, she must commit a significant portion of her time to the effort. In some of the larger private university settings, this might amount to more than half of the director's time.

If she makes this time commitment to fundraising, the director will not be able also to function as an operational head. Fundraising, though it can be fun, can also be intense and exhausting work. It requires evenings, weekends, lunches, off-site meetings, and travel. It is necessary to have confidence in one's subordinates so that daily library operations can be left in their hands. A pathfinding leader recognizes that this approach does not undermine her authority.

2. *Establish a few firm priorities.* In order to focus the vision and leadership of the development efforts the library director must ask, "What are the two or three most important fundraising priorities in my library?" There will be many needs that any library will have at any given time. If the librarian is to be a successful fundraiser, however, she must prioritize those needs. She must be able to speak concisely, convincingly, and enthusiastically about their urgency. She must be able to convince others of their importance. We cannot stress this point too strongly: vacillation on the issue of priorities is deadly to a development effort. Both the director's colleagues in the parent institution and prospective donors need to receive a clear and consistent message about what is most important. Clarity of vision is imperative. A leader must know where her library is going and what is most essential to getting it there.

PERSONALITY

Personality is not an easy topic to discuss. What could be more personal than personality? And what is more difficult than seeing ourselves? But a clear sense of oneself is necessary in order to be able to design a fundraising program that will be successful. Just as the Leavitt management model aids us in understanding leadership abilities, so the Myers-Briggs personality inventory can help us assess key information about how we relate to others. On diskette this survey is known as *Please Understand Me* and takes only about 30 minutes to complete.[4]

The original creators of the test, Katharine C. Briggs and her daughter Isabel Briggs Myers, were interested in developing an instrument that would bridge gaps in human understanding.[5] Their test, called the Myers-Briggs Type Indicator (MBTI) is based on Jungian theories of personality. Daryl Sharp, writing about this test, describes how he used it to evaluate his own personality:

> Being consciously aware of the way I tend to function makes it possible for me to assess my attitudes and behavior in a given situation and adjust them accordingly. It enables me both to compensate for my personal disposition and to be tolerant of someone who does not function as I do—someone who has, perhaps, a strength or facility I myself lack.[6]

For many people the Myers-Briggs test promotes greater self-understanding, helping them to recognize basic patterns and tendencies in the way they relate to the world. The test consists of four pairings of "preference strengths." The first pairing compares Introversion (I) and Extraversion (sic) (E). People who rate high on the scale for extroversion direct their energy outward and are energized when people are around. They prefer verbal communication and like to "think out loud." In contrast, introverts are stimulated by the inner world of ideas and sometimes experience a drain on their energy from too much personal contact. They prefer written communication and like to think through ideas before they talk about them.

The second pairing assesses how the subject perceives the world around him. A high score on the Sensing (S) scale suggests that one prefers working with known facts—with procedures, outlines, and plans—while iNtuitives (Ns) look for possibilities and relationships and "often leap mysteriously beyond the concrete in their perceptions."[7]

The next pairing looks at one's preference for methods of making decisions. Thinkers (Ts) make their decisions objectively, logically, and impersonally. Feelers (Fs) tend to make judgments more subjectively, based on personal and social values.

The final MBTI pairing compares the life-styles of Judgers (Js) and Perceivers (Ps). A high J rating indicates a preference for a planned, decided, orderly way of life as opposed to the more flexible, spontaneous way of life valued by those with a high rating on the P scale.

After the results are tabulated, the subject is given a four-part description of his personality type from among 16 different possibilities. The Center for the Application of Psychological Type (CAPT) has compiled a useful data base of 250,000 people who have taken the test. Of these, 267 people listed "librarian" as their profession. The librarians revealed an overall preference to be Introverted (61 percent), Sensing (54 percent), Feeling (67 percent), and Judging (64 percent). These ISFJs, who make up only 6 percent of the U.S. population, are "well-organized fact gatherers, quiet, calm, reflective, dependable, and patient with particulars and procedures."[8] Other MBTI workshops have confirmed that most librarians are ISFJs, but that most library managers are INFJs.

Slightly extroverted, intuitive individuals who score high on the Feeling scale (ENFs) make excellent fundraisers. They are adept at building relationships with individuals and groups. They have an uncanny ability to sense peoples' needs and desires. They love nothing more than to go into a room full of strangers and tell them about their cause. At the same time, they are sincerely interested in how other people see the world.

In contrast, introverted individuals who prefer to work with known facts rather than relationships and possibilities, and who prefer impersonal analysis and logic to feelings, are not as well-equipped to raise money. Giving is often emotional, and these individuals are disturbed by emotion. They prefer guidelines and instructions on how to deal with things; fundraising is imprecise and unpredictable. Socializing frequently strikes them as a waste of time. ISTs see their problems as their own; communicating about problems, much less asking others for help in solving them, seems to them weak and inappropriate.

In general, then, librarianship and fundraising seem to attract very different personality types. Small wonder that most librarians don't want to be fundraisers (and that most fundraisers don't want to be librarians). Fortunately, most librarians don't have to be fundraisers, but those who want to be library leaders *do* have to be. Is it hopeless? Of course not. Where personality is concerned, there is a middle ground between being very well-equipped and very ill-equipped to raise money. For many people, fundraising offers the chance to break out of customary patterns. Where logic and analysis have been the hallmarks of one's style, now one can develop an ability to be spontaneous and intuitive; where one felt safe with the concrete, one can develop a flair for the abstract. Fundraising offers a chance for growth, both institutionally and personally. As Daryl Sharp observes:

> From this point of view, the important question is . . . in *this* situation or with *that* person, how did I function? With what effect? Did my actions and the way I expressed myself truly reflect my judgments (thinking and feeling) and perception (sensation and intuition)? And if not, why not? . . . How and why did I mess things up? What does this say about my psychology? What can I do about it? What do I *want* to do about it?[9]

Often, library directors will work with development officers and, though they may be different personality types, both can benefit from their partnership. As Isabel Briggs Myers points out:

> Opposite types can complement each other in any joint undertaking. When two people approach a problem from opposite sides, each sees things not visible to the other. When opposites must work or live together, an understanding of type does much to lessen the friction. Disagreement is less irritating when you recognize it would hardly be normal for the other person to agree. He or she is not being willfully contrary, but is simply being an opposite type. Opposite types can be tremendously useful to each other when given the chance.[10]

ASSESSING YOUR FUNDRAISING POTENTIAL

Having assessed his personality, how does a library director know if he is ready to take on a large-scale fundraising effort? A library director can look at his success with other key constituent groups as test areas before embarking on an ambitious fundraising program. If he can successfully galvanize their support, then it is likely that he will be able to raise a good deal of money.

1. *Can the library director successfully make the case for the library to the prevailing power structures (e.g., the senior administration of a university or other parent institution, the city council, the state legislature and administration)?* If the director can successfully promote his vision to the prevailing power structure, he will probably be successful with other external constituencies. If, however, the library is a step-child and the leaders of the organization—the trustees, university president, legislators, and others—do not see the library's well-being as essential to their own well-being, the director must first try to change this attitude. He must persuade them that the excellence of the library goes hand-in-hand with the excellence of all concerned.

If he is unable to overcome this unfortunate attitude, it might be well to think twice before embarking on a large-scale fundraising endeavor. Without the support of the power structure, without the clear endorsement of the library as a priority, major-gift fundraising will be a difficult, if not impossible, endeavor.

2. *In the unique case of academic libraries, can the library director galvanize the central development office?* The central development office takes its marching orders from the university administration; therefore, persuading the administration of the library's mission should facilitate the support of central development. If the university administration does not back the library, however, neither will the central development office in most cases. But even assuming that he has the university administration's backing, the library director will still need to be able to make the case for the library to the central development office. Without the library director's intervention, the development office will probably consider the library to be one of the least promising areas for support. Rallying this support is not a job the director can pass off to his development officer; it is *his* job as library director.

3. *Does the director have contacts and create them in the community?* If he does not, and if he is unwilling to make the requisite effort to make them (if the whole idea of going out into the community seems unimportant or insurmountably unnerving and bewildering), this should be taken into account in deciding whether to go ahead with a full-scale program.

Successful fundraisers are attuned to people and make contacts constantly, in every sphere in which they move. They are effective *boundary spanners*, to use a term from the field of organizational behavior, in that they transfer information interpersonally across organizational boundaries.[11] For example, a boundary-spanning librarian would know, and be known, by book dealers, leading vendors, collectors, library leaders, educators, scholars, and writers. These librarians take advantage of every opportunity to talk about their cause, about the exciting, wonderful chance they are lucky enough to have, to be running a library engaged in new programs and important educational missions. And they will not hesitate to name, at every appropriate occasion, their two or three top priorities for development, priorities that supply wonderful opportunities for prospective donors.

One good way to make contacts is for librarians to be out serving their community in addition to asking others to serve their cause. They too should be on boards and should serve in volunteer capacities for worthy projects. Not only is this equitable, but it is also good for the library's image and is an excellent way to make contacts with other civic-minded people.

YOUR FUNDRAISING STYLE

How you go about development will in large part depend on your personal style. By knowing yourself—your strengths and weaknesses, likes and dislikes—it will be easier for you to find a fundraising style that works well for you. For example, some people enjoy dining, so they do well organizing their development events around meals. Others prefer to structure their contact with people more formally, along the lines of business meetings. Some people shine before a large audience, others are masters at one-on-one encounters, and others come alive at parties. Think about what situations energize and suit you, and create your style to take maximum advantage of these. Fashion your program in a way that allows you to shine.

NOTES

1. Harold J. Leavitt, *Corporate Pathfinders* (New York: Viking Penguin, 1986), passim.

2. We use the term *associate director* generically to encompass, in the public library setting, senior librarians, and, in the university library setting, assistant/associate university librarians.

3. A. Westly Rowland, *Key Resources on Institutional Advancement* (San Francisco: Jossey-Bass, 1986), pp. 190–195. Also Margaret A. Duronio and Bruce A. Loessin, *Effective Fund Raising in Higher Education* (San Francisco: Jossey-Bass, 1991), pp. 198–199.

4. Douglas Dean, *Please Understand Me* (Charleston, W. Va.: Cambridge Career Products, May 1986).

5. Barbara Webb, "Type-casting: Life with Myers-Briggs," *Library Journal* 115 (June 15, 1990): 32–37.

6. Daryl Sharp, *Personality Types: Jung's Model of Typology* (Toronto: Inner City Books, 1987), p. 91.

7. Webb, p. 35.

8. Ibid., p. 34.

9. Sharp, pp. 91–92.

10. Isabel Briggs Myers, *Introduction to Type* (Palo Alto, Calif.: Consulting Psychologists Press, 1987), p. 26.

11. R. T. Keller, A. D. Szilagyi, and W. E. Holland, "Boundary Spanning Activity and Employee Reactions," *Human Relations* 29 (July 1976): 700.

CHAPTER 2 **Basic Concepts**
The Art and Science of Fundraising

Now that we have examined the relationship between fundraising and you, we are ready to introduce the basic concepts of fundraising. To facilitate the discussion, we have divided these concepts into two camps, the science and the art of fundraising. The science of fundraising includes those concepts that reveal regular patterns and cycles, so, in that way, they can be considered "scientific." [1] For example, fundraisers see that some people have certain attributes that qualify them as good prospects for giving to their organization. As the fundraisers nurture relationships with these "prospects," the relationships can be charted as moving through a process of cultivation that leads to solicitation and, when appropriate, resolicitation. By identifying such patterns, establishing common terms, and describing other basic concepts of fundraising, we can demystify the process to some extent.

The art of fundraising, on the other hand, is highly situational and relies on good instincts, an understanding of donor psychology, and other unquantifiable abilities. The art of fundraising is difficult to analyze, which may account for its not being dealt with in many books and articles. This art is critical, however, to successful fundraising, since it resists the tendency to view people (and to treat them) as so many objects gliding along on a conveyor belt toward solicitation. The term *art* more fully describes the challenges, difficulties, and rewards of fundraising.

THE SCIENCE OF FUNDRAISING

Before proceeding, it may be well to begin this section with a definition and description of successful library development. *Library development is a carefully orchestrated, purposive effort to raise substantial sums of money by identifying and cultivating potential donors and by soliciting gifts from them when their goals and wishes are congruent with the library's goals and priorities. The goal of the development program is to enhance the library's independence. Therefore, fundraising is judged to be effective not principally on the basis of dollars raised, but to the extent that gifts contribute to the strategic vision for the library. Successful fundraising depends on the leadership and participation of the library director.* For purposes of the discussion in this chapter, we assume adequate levels of staffing to support the development program; matters of staffing are fully described in the next chapter.

The basic vocabulary of fundraising concerns donors and potential donors. Potential donors are referred to as *prospects*. The universe of prospects can be further differentiated: if little or nothing is known of a prospect, she is sometimes called a *suspect*. When a relationship has been established with a prospect, the prospect is said to be in *cultivation*. Past donors are prospects, too, if you think they will make additional gifts. Established donors, especially if they participate actively in the organization, are called *volunteers*.

The MAGIC Ingredients

How do you recognize a prospect? Professional fundraisers evaluate prospects by asking a series of questions, which we have formulated into the mnemonic MAGIC:

M   Does the prospect have **means**?
A   What is the person's **age** and are there heirs?
G   Is the person a **giver**?
I   Is the person **involved** in your organization?
C   Does the person have **contacts**?

A person must have either personal means or contacts in order to be a valid prospect. By "contacts" we mean more than simply knowing people; we mean that the person is in a position to give away other peoples' money—through membership on a philanthropic board, for example. Assuming that prospects have means or contacts, it is necessary to find out if they are givers. There are a number of ways to find out about a person's giving history. If you are in a university, your development office can tell you about the prospect's record of giving to your institution. If the person is highly visible in the community or has a personal foundation, the development office's staff can also research a person's public giving patterns. Another way to find out about a prospect's giving is simply to talk with the person informally about his or her community involvements.

Age is an important issue because most people who give, do so in their 50s and 60s. In this key age bracket, a person without heirs who has means can often be an excellent prospect. Involvement is also essential. A person must have some reasonable tie to your organization in order to be a viable prospect.

Prospects are seen as moving through a six-step *development cycle* (see figure 1). In the first step, a prospect (or at this stage, a suspect) is identified. The second step consists of involving the prospect in the organization, whether through an invitation to an event, a board appointment, or a lunch date. Orchestrated involvement is known as cultivation, and it can last for months or years. Cultivation leads to solicitation, or asking the prospect to make a gift. A successful solicitation is followed by stewardship, or the careful nurturing and continuing involvement of donors. Careful stewardship leads to resolicitation.

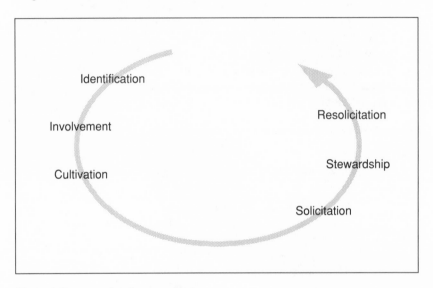

Figure 1. Prospect development cycle

The development cycle holds true for almost all major gifts. It even holds true, with slight variations, for gifts that seem to come from out of the blue—the process was going on, but nobody knew about it. In these instances, the process might look more like this: the prospect sees himself as someone who has the means to make a gift and is interested in doing so; he identifies himself. He may or may not get involved in the organization (the cultivation step). He elects to make a gift, soliciting himself, in effect. The organization responds gratefully (the stewardship step), the donor likes it, and he eventually makes another gift. This pattern also holds for bequests except, obviously, for the last step: resolicitation.

The most significant exception to the model involves memorial gifts. Memorial gifts, which account for a large percentage of giving, essentially bypass the early stages of the cycle. They are an emotional and healing response to a painful occurrence: the death of a loved one. In these instances, the donor comes to you. Though such donors bypass the early stages of the cycle, they frequently require sensitive stewardship. Resolicitation, however, is usually not possible.

The development cycle takes time. One rule of thumb is that the typical major gift requires thirteen contacts over the space of two to three years. Many development professionals managing a large number of prospects think of the cycle as requiring about three years. "Megagifts" take much longer. One fundraiser, when asked how she obtained a $20 million gift for her university, replied, "Simple. We cultivated the donor for twenty years." Multimillion-dollar gifts almost invariably involve long-term relationships.

Organizing Fundraising

Fundraisers commonly think of donors and prospective donors as falling into one of two camps: annual givers or major givers. Just as librarians sometimes have thought of themselves as being in either public services or technical services, development professionals will often identify themselves with major gifts or with (as they would say) annual funds.

Why is the distinction between major giving and annual giving important? There are three reasons. First, as we said above, there is usually a division of labor along the lines of major giving on the one hand and middle-range and annual giving on the other. Just as it would not be appropriate for someone in technical services to be concerned with service guidelines for the reference department, so it would not be appropriate for someone you had hired to do major gifts work to be concerned, in more than a general way, with direct mail or with the Friends of the Library group.

The second reason for understanding the important distinction between annual giving and major giving is that it is basic to thinking about prospects. In assessing prospects' potentials, you are really asking in which camp they belong. Should they be cultivated by means of the Friends or should they receive individualized attention? If they should receive the latter, what is your next step in cultivating the relationship?

The third and most important reason has to do with how the library director, as the head fundraiser, prioritizes her time. If the library has an ambitious development program, the director will want to give highest priority to major-gift prospects; she will not want to be too concerned with, say, building the membership of the Friends or overseeing mail appeals.

Annual Giving

Most of us are annual givers: people who make gifts, generally in the $50 to $100 range, in response to periodic (not necessarily annual) appeals such as those from educational television and local privately supported radio stations in on-air pledge drives. We also give in response to mail appeals, known in the fundraising business as "direct mail." There is a seemingly endless number of nonprofit organizations that use direct mail, including museums, zoos, environmental organizations, literacy promoters, universities, and library Friends groups. Telemarketing is another string in the annual fund bow; many of us have grown accustomed to receiving yearly phone calls from the annual funds of our alma maters. Door-to-door solicitation, an approach perfected by the Girl Scouts, is another method used to raise large numbers of low-level contributions.

Major Giving

Major gifts are multithousand-dollar gifts. There is no hard-and-fast dollar figure attached to a major gift because such gifts should be assessed relative to the range of gifts an organization normally receives. A small public library might consider $10,000 a major gift. New York Public Library might think of a major gift as being $100,000. Most fundraisers think of $25,000 as being an arbitrary minimum level for a major gift. Major gifts are made (1) after a significant period of one-on-one cultivation, (2) after the careful formulation of a strategy for the prospect, and (3) after the prospect has been asked directly to make a gift by the most prestigious, effective, and appropriate person or persons connected with an organization. In the case of university libraries, one of these solicitors will usually be the library director. Contrary to popular belief, professional fundraisers rarely ask people for money. Remember, they are Sherpa guides. The fundraiser's role is to help the library director meet, get to know, and effectively solicit major-donor prospects. The differences between annual gifts and major gifts may be summarized as follows.

Annual Gifts	Major Gifts
Made each year up to about $5,000 per year	A commitment of significant resources that may be pledged in installments
Cash	Cash, appreciated assets, real estate, or a planned-giving vehicle
Solicited each year	Solicited over time based on the donor's circumstances
Solicited by phone, mail, or by a volunteer or staff member	Solicited in person and often with a fully developed proposal

Middle-Range Giving

A middle area exists between a true annual giver and a major giver; this range usually falls between $100 and $10,000 for most types of libraries. Givers in the middle range may be either generous annual givers who really do not have the ability or inclination to give more, or they may be potential major donors who are not yet making gifts of great size. For this reason, donors who fall into this category should receive special attention. Research and assess, as thoroughly as possible, the potential of middle-range donors to give larger gifts, and be sure that they receive attention from both the library director and the development staff member in charge of annual giving.

Support Groups: The Fundraising Swimming Pool

In fundraising terminology, a Friends of the Library organization is a support group. In a small-scale fundraising program with no major-gift effort, the Friends may be the entire fundraising effort, forming the annual fund for the library and providing events and publications for its members. In a full-scale program with annual, middle-range, and major giving, the Friends group will loom less large, but even here it can function as an important element in the development cycle. An analogy demonstrates this role and also provides a way of showing how different types of givers fit into a development program.

A Friends group is like a swimming pool. Most people, the annual givers (i.e., the Friends themselves), enter the pool from the shallow end. Major givers enter the pool from the deep end. Both groups get into the pool by virtue of having made a gift. The Friends provide a place for both to swim: the pool provides a mechanism for the cultivation and stewardship phases of the development cycle. Sometimes a Friend—who entered from the shallow end by virtue of a relatively small gift—will swim all the way to the deep end and make a major gift; sometimes a Friend from the deep end will swim to the shallow end and persuade one of the annual givers to cross to the deep end. Provided that the Friends are geared to serve a development purpose, and provided that their activities and events are fun and stimulating, they can be invaluable in providing a vehicle for involvement (more about this in Chapter 6).

Working with Prospects

Now that we have established some basic vocabulary, concepts, and models, we are ready to discuss the initial question you might ask about prospects.

Who Will Give to My Library?

One thing is certain: *the vast majority of large gifts will come from a relatively small number of individual donors, most of whom will already be known to you or to your organization.* The simplicity of this idea belies its importance. For example, you may be barraged with ideas from well-meaning people who are certain you are overlooking a number of obvious prospects, or that your base of donors is not "broad enough." Your librarians may ask why you are not "going after" a particular foundation or corporation, especially one that they may have read about recently in the press. And your donors will sometimes insist that you approach some well-known public figure whom you do not know at all and whose interest in your cause is doubtful at best. We call this the "Why don't you call Donald Trump?" syndrome. (In earlier years this phenomenon might have been "Why don't you call King Midas, Croesus, Andrew Carnegie, John D. Rockefeller, Howard Hughes, or J. Paul Getty?" The names change, but the phenomenon does not.)

The vast majority of large gifts will come from a relatively small number of individual donors. It is commonly said in fundraising that 80 percent of the total money you receive will be donated by 20 percent of your donors. Recent research has shown that, increasingly, more of the overall money being raised is coming from fewer donors, to the point where as much as 90 percent of a campaign goal can come from as few as 10 percent of the total donors to a campaign.[2]

The conclusion to draw from this data is that you can expect your library fundraising to reflect a similar pattern. Do not expect that a large number of little donors will be responsible for most of your gifts. People who do not understand this 90–10 phenomenon will often suggest that a fundraising goal be divided into equal shares and parceled out among a number of prospects. They will say, "Let's divide this $1,000,000 goal into 10 equal shares of $100,000. That way, we only have to find 10 donors. Simple!" Unfortunately fundraising does not work that way.

Most donors will be individuals who are already known to you or your organization. The donor prospect target, illustrated in figure 2, indicates by a series of concentric rings who is most likely to give, less likely to give, and least likely to give to your library. In the bull's-eye are your best prospects; as you proceed outward through the successive rings, the prospects are less and less likely to respond to your appeals. As a fundraiser, you are not looking to make a convert out of a nonbeliever—someone in the outer ring. Indeed, as far as conversion goes, you are mainly looking for people who already believe in your cause on some level. Therefore, your energies should be directed—in addition to looking after your past donors—to bringing into the fold people who have demonstrated an interest in libraries, books, and learning.

Corporations and well-known high rollers are unlikely to be significant benefactors. Corporate and foundation giving together account for only 10 percent of all charitable giving in our country; gifts from individuals,

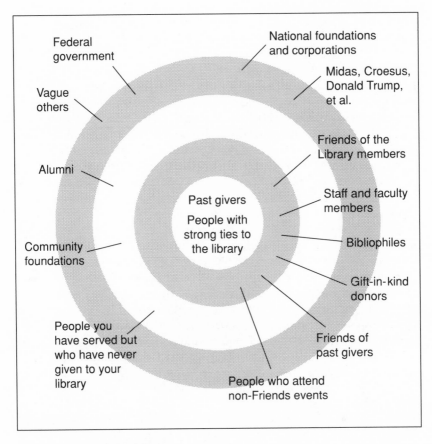

Figure 2. Donor prospect target

including bequests, account for 90 percent.[3] The donor group to your library will reflect this, and your concentration on priority prospects should too. Even foundations or corporations that do contribute to an organization generally do so at the direction of individuals within them who have clout.

Major donors rarely come from the large category of "vague others." Though it is sometimes possible, with careful planning and the right connections, to recruit some of these vague others who have no ties at all to your organization, they are not usually good prospects. Your most important prospects, then, are people who are involved in your library and especially those who have given to you in the past. Individuals are the key; devote your efforts to those who care about your library. The time that you expend on them, as opposed to foundations and corporations and vague others, should reflect your awareness that as much as 90 percent of your support will come from them and that individuals are, moreover, the keys to foundation and corporation giving as well.

There is a category of prospect who is the opposite of a vague other. For lack of a better term, this is the "busybody." Busybodies are usually small-time donors, but they command and expect the attentions normally given to a major-gift prospect. Busybodies typically take your time with leads that turn out to be worthless, think they know better than you do what directions the library should be taking, and may frequently refer to their "wills." In working with busybodies, be particularly sure of your purposes and niche (ideas that will be discussed in detail in Chapter 4), and be willing to draw the line with them. In the final analysis, establishing some distance from such individuals is sometimes not a bad idea.

You can test the validity of the donor prospect target yourself by thinking about how you respond to the voluminous quantities of direct mail that you receive personally. You probably throw a good deal of it away without even opening it, but every so often a piece will arrive that coincides with some feelings you have about a given issue, whether it is handgun control, civil rights, or an environmental concern. Whatever it is, you decide you *must* support that cause, and you write a check. Professionals who solicit contributions through the mail understand perfectly the way these donations come about. They are not trying to convince everyone of the worthiness of their cause; they are simply trying to find those people who, to some extent, believe in it already.

How Do I Ask Them?

The donor prospect target also provides a useful framework for beginning to think about your solicitation methods as they relate to your prospects, whichever circle they are in. The solicitation methods you have available to you, from most personal to least personal, are: (1) face-to-face (whether with an individual or group); (2) telephone (or with groups, telemarketing); and (3) mail (or with large groups, direct mail). Whenever you are trying to get a message across, the more personal the method, the more effective it is. Since it is impossible to deliver every solicitation personally, you should vary your approach from most personal to least personal as you move from your best prospects in the inner circle to your least likely prospects in the outer rings.

For example, though many people may normally detest receiving telephone solicitations, when you receive a call from an enthusiastic eighteen-year-old from your alma mater, you may find that you are disarmed and that it is practically impossible to turn the student down. By virtue of its being more personal, telemarketing is usually more effective than direct mail; it is far more difficult to say no to a person than it is to crumple a letter.

Fundraisers know that telemarketing is best applied to that category of prospects for whom it will be most effective. They would not, of course, phone their established major donors—the innermost ring of their own concentric circles—about making a small gift. Rather, within the university setting, for example, telemarketing is used to contact a certain category of alumni who may or may not have previously responded to a telemarketing or direct-mail solicitation, but who in any case can be expected to have some degree of interest in the university and some means with which to make a modest gift.

When fundraisers use direct mail to target those prospects in the outer circles, they try to overcome the handicap of this least personal of all solicitation methods by making their letters as personal as possible. Toward that end, they will sometimes customize their letters to incorporate the recipient's name not only into the salutation but also into the body of the letter. They will also write the letters in the second person in the most immediate manner and most engaging tone possible. Direct-mail marketers also use every trick at their disposal to get you to open the piece and to read it. They know, for example, that the eye will scan the salutation area and pause for a postscript. That is why you will rarely see a direct mail piece without a P.S.

To What Will They Give?

As we said in Chapter 1, people give to big ideas, to bold and exciting plans. Prospects will be drawn to the idea of a whole new kind of library or a library that establishes a collection for their special area of interest, particularly if it is the first of its type. Donors are not usually drawn to projects that appear to involve ongoing operations (e.g., retrospective conversion) or that appear to be huge and insurmountable (e.g., preserving the general collections of the library).

Donors give to satisfy their needs rather than the library's needs, and donors' needs usually involve projects that will "make a difference" rather than projects designed to maintain already established resources in the library. If there is any exception, it is that most donors understand the need for funds to support book purchases; but projects concerning other ongoing needs have little appeal.

If you decide that what your library most needs is retrospective conversion, preservation, or facilities improvements, you will have to be very creative in packaging these opportunities. For example, you might design a gift opportunity involving the creation of a conservation treatment laboratory. Your package would allow you to name the facility for the donor, and it would emphasize the "big idea" behind preservation, namely, preserving

our culture's written record. The proposal might include dramatic illustra-
tions of before-and-after treatments. The opportunity should be specific
and carry a finite price tag—attributes that make it attractive to donors.

Some projects, no matter how important they are to *you,* cannot be
glamorized for your donors. No amount of creativity will overcome their
lack of appeal. Retrospective conversion is perhaps in this category.
Though it is important to many libraries, it offers nothing tangible to
donors: the results of the project are stored away in computer memories.
Trying to disguise projects of this sort may hurt your credibility with
donors. Though it is sometimes possible to work with donors to bring their
needs exactly into line with the library's needs, sometimes the adjustment
is not possible. When developing gift opportunities, remember that you
are trying to serve the donor's needs and interests as well as your own.

Gift opportunities usually take the form of a brief written proposal
tailored to the person who will receive it. The substance of the proposal is
presented in person; the document's purpose is to serve as a summary and
follow-up to the verbal presentation. Since a gift opportunity emphasizes a
big idea, it is quite different from a grant proposal, which spells out all the
details and minutiae of a project. It will be written (usually by your development director) with the idea of achieving congruence between the
library's interests (why you want and need the gift) and the potential
donors' interests (why they might want to make the gift).

How Do I Thank Them?

People give to worthwhile projects and to attractive gift opportunities, but
they also give to be recognized for their giving. Recognition for most major
donors goes far beyond mere expressions of thanks. Most major donors want
to see their names placed on something: on a bookplate, on the arch of a
room, on a piece of equipment, or on a plaque on a wall along with the names
of other donors. The need to attach a donor's name to a gift opportunity is so
important that "naming opportunities" are part-and-parcel of gift opportunities, and fundraisers think about naming opportunities as they design gift
opportunities.

It should go without saying that, in embarking on a library development
program having a major-gifts component, the director must be prepared to
provide suitable forms of recognition. Few librarians have difficulty with
the idea of naming funds for donors, but it seems that some have a great
reluctance to provide more tangible forms of recognition. This is a problem, since it is these tangible forms of recognition that often motivate
givers. Therefore, if you wish to have a high-stakes development program,
you must be prepared to attach your donors' names to rooms, to branch
libraries, and even to the main library itself.

Many donors also expect to be made to feel important and to be accorded special privileges. They get this VIP treatment regularly from all the people and organizations that are courting them for gifts. In the university setting, major donors and prospective donors are not paying for their football tickets, their parking permits, or most of their meals on campus. It is important to know this so you will be prepared for requests from donors and prospective donors for special library privileges, parking arrangements, and, in a university situation, help with student admissions. It is up to you how to respond to these requests and to know where to draw the lines. But be aware of the expectations of donors and the treatment they are likely accorded by other institutions or departments within your own institution. Remember that, in embarking on a development program, you are sending a signal to prospective donors that you are playing the "cultivation game." If you refuse to grant a particular request, your prospects may disqualify you from play. Sometimes it is helpful to recognize that some requests (such as courtesy parking) are harmless and easy; others are dangerous and difficult (such as those that involve requests for titles, office space, and even token salaries in connection with a gift). Library privileges are among the things that are uniquely yours to give away, and we think you should. In truth, very few of your donors will actually use their borrowing privileges. Draw your lines where they really matter.

THE ART OF FUNDRAISING

The art of fundraising involves a sense of what motivates giving, an understanding of donor psychology, and an appreciation of the importance of strategy. Mastery of the art means a grasp of the subtleties of human values, needs, attitudes, and behavior as they relate to philanthropy.

Donor Psychology

Motivations for giving are complex. People's reasons for giving are highly personal, unique to each individual, and closely linked to their values and attitudes, elements that make up a person's mind-set. In the end, most people give for what they think giving will do for *them*, not for what it will do for *you*. Donors' giving behaviors are based on a combination of thoughts and emotions, their past experiences with giving, and a sense of proper timing, either financially or otherwise. These motivating factors are seldom entirely understood or recognized by the donors, and they often intersect and overlap. Your job is to be attuned to your donor prospects, to really listen (not just with your ears but also with your intuition) to what makes them tick.

Abraham Maslow's hierarchy of needs identifies people's basic needs as being for water, food, shelter, sleep, and sex. Next comes the need for safety and security. After these needs are satisfied, individuals seek to satisfy their needs for love and belonging, for self-esteem and esteem from others. For this reason, fundraising appeals often emphasize the benefit of belonging and of becoming part of the "family." They also satisfy the donor's need for self-esteem and esteem from others. Such benefits make donors feel proud of having supported a worthy cause, and they usually offer donors some kind of public recognition for their support.

Harold Seymour, author of a well-known book in the fundraising field, identifies two motivations for giving.[4] He believes that there are two universal aspirations: first, "to be sought," to feel that we are valuable to someone or something external to ourselves, and, second, to be "a worthwhile member of a worthwhile group," to feel a pride in our association with and contributions to an organization or community that itself is vital and merits admiration.

If people give in order to fulfill certain basic needs, they also do so in order to express how they see themselves in relation to the world. Many people who give do so out of a sense of duty. They feel they have profited from their work in the community, and they want to give something back. They feel a moral obligation. Some people who give do so because it gives them a sense of pleasure. Such people feel a personal pride and involvement in their benefactions. Many givers have a spiritual or mystical idea of giving. They may believe that if they give, they will get back.

Why do people give to a particular institution? Belief in the mission of the institution is the most important factor in motivating a major gift. Without an interest in the organization or what it is trying to accomplish, a person will never make a gift, no matter how exciting the organization's projects are or how charismatic its askers. Closely linked to belief in the organization is confidence in and regard for its leader. As we have said, donors respond to dynamic and visionary leaders. They want to be inspired. Third, givers' perceptions of the financial stability of the institution affect their ideas about the institution's mission and its leaders. People usually give to stable organizations, not to troubled ones.

Beyond their belief in the mission of the institution and the vision of its leader, givers consider other factors when contemplating a gift. For one thing, donors want to go with winners. They often give to a program because others are giving to it; few donors want to go it alone. They give to opportunities, not needs, and they give to programs where they feel they can make a difference.

Ego frequently plays a part in giving. Many philanthropists are inspired by the wish, perhaps common to everyone, to immortalize themselves.

Even though they may tell you otherwise, many donors also crave adulation. Successful fundraisers know that it is wise not to underestimate a person's need for self-aggrandizement.

Finally—and this point cannot be emphasized too strongly—donors give if asked to give but do not give if they are not asked. When all is said and done, the number one reason people give is because they are asked. Potential donors do not read your mind or respond to hints. They must be asked directly for a specific gift.

Donor Strategy

Now that we have a sense of what motivates giving and some understanding of basic donor psychology, we can turn to the issue of donor strategy. Developing strategies for communicating with prospects is the heart of fundraising. Research about how people communicate, generally referred to as communication theory, illuminates the four variables of donor strategy. For example, some communication researchers have organized their studies around the query: "*Who* says *what* to *whom* using what *method* with what *effect*?" Modified for fundraising communication, the question becomes "Who *asks* what of whom using what method with what effect?" In terms used by communication theorists, the person asking for the gift is in the role of the message *source,* the description of the gift opportunity is the *message* itself, the prospect is the *recipient* of the message, and the method by which "the ask" is made is called the message *channel.*[5]

Though most fundraisers do not use the vocabulary of communication theory, these four elements are, in fact, precisely the ones used by people formulating solicitation strategies. When fundraising staff members meet, they discuss four variables as they relate to each prospect. They strategize about (1) who should ask the prospect for the gift, (2) what form the gift opportunity should take, (3) the method to be used to ask the prospect, and (4) the unique characteristics of the prospect.[6] For example, let us describe a hypothetical strategy meeting at a university to discuss Mr. and Mrs. Prospect. The Prospects have no specific intellectual interests. However, they have a child attending the university, are looking for a charity to support, and would like to associate themselves with an academic institution. The meeting of the university's development team to discuss the strategy for the solicitation might go something like this:

Q. What would make a good gift opportunity for the Prospects?
A. They would respond well to something that we could attach their name to.

Q. Why would they respond well to that?
A. Because they would enjoy public recognition for their contribution.

Q. What magnitude of gift are they capable of?

A. Our research shows that they could make a seven-figure gift.

Q. How about naming a prominent room in our new library building after them?

A. That would be perfect; they find the idea of libraries tremendously empowering and enriching.

Q. Are they ready to be asked?

A. No, they need more cultivation.

Q. What form should this take and what should our timetable be?

A. Cultivation should be at the highest level and take the form of intimate gatherings. Once every three months at least, the director should see them for lunch or dinner; we will also want to involve the president. Either the president or the director should solicit them in about a year, depending on how the relationships mature.

The fundraisers have formulated a basic strategy for the Prospects. When it becomes time to ask the Prospects for a gift, the fundraisers once again will discuss them with reference to the four variables: who asks, for what and for how much, by what method, and what unique characteristics about them are most pertinent? Since the fundraisers are discussing a major gift, the method would always be face-to-face; but the specifics of where the message might be delivered and under what circumstances would be matters for careful consideration. These are discussed in detail in Chapter 5.

This paradigm works for annual giving also. Say, for example, that you want to recruit a new Friends member whom you think may have potential for a major gift. Who invites the prospect to join? How—by letter or phone? At what giving level should he be asked to join? What makes you think he will respond favorably?

As a library director, you are frequently the message source. And you have going for you the two most important characteristics that make your message persuasive to others: expertise and trustworthiness. When a message's recipients see its source as expert, attractive, or successful, they are usually more likely to be swayed. People want to believe in the expertise, authority, competence, and status of someone in a position of power.

In order to earn someone's trust, you must have credibility. Credibility consists of four elements: your experience, your knowledge, the way you present yourself, and your associations.[7] Your experience has brought you to your position, your track record has withstood the scrutiny of the formal selection process, and your personal qualities have held up under the scrutiny of the "off-the-record" selection process. Your knowledge, from the point of view of your prospects, will primarily involve your academic background—the schools you attended, your advanced degrees; most donors will not be much impressed by your publications or prominence in professional organizations. Your presentation involves your appearance, the way you speak, your personality, and your professional demeanor. Lastly, your associations—your connections—can help establish introductory and temporary trust in situations where you would not otherwise have it. In Chapter 5 we will have more to say about earning credibility when you find yourself in one-on-one situations with donors.

Art and science, magic and technique, inspiration and application—these are the elements of successful fundraising. You will blend these elements in your unique way as you build your development team and find your niche, topics to which we will turn next.

NOTES

1. We are not suggesting that there is a "science" of fundraising in any literal sense. Rather we use "science" here figuratively for purposes of contrast.

2. Kathleen S. Kelly, *Fund Raising and Public Relations: A Critical Analysis* (Hillsdale, N.J.: Lawrence Erlbaum, 1991), pp. 278–279.

3. American Association of Fund-Raising Council (AAFRC) Trust for Philanthropy, *Giving USA: The Annual Report on Philanthropy for the Year 1989* (New York: American Association of Fund-Raising Council, 1990), p. 6.

4. Harold Seymour, *Designs for Fund-Raising* (New York: McGraw-Hill, 1966), p. 6.

5. These elements of communication were first described in this way by Bruce Lannes Smith, Harold Lasswell, and Ralph D. Casey in *Propaganda, Communication, and Public Opinion: A Comprehensive Reference Guide* (Princeton N.J.: Princeton University Press, 1946), p. 3. For an overview of these elements and research on related factors that affect communication, see Richard E. Petty and John T. Cacioppo, *Attitudes and Persuasion—Classic and Contemporary Approaches* (Dubuque, Iowa: Wm. C. Brown Co., 1981), pp. 60–94.

6. An oft-repeated development adage reduces fundraising to "selecting the right person to ask the right person, the right way, for the right amount, for the right reason, at the right time." See Fisher Howe, "What You Need to Know about Fund Raising," *Harvard Business Review* 63(2) (March-April 1985): 18–21. We tend to be in sympathy with the commentator who likened this advice to "buying stocks that only go up"; that is, we find this formula both pat and imprecise, and prefer to use communication theory in discussing donor strategy.

7. These elements of credibility are identified by Robert B. Miller and Stephen E. Heiman in *Conceptual Selling* (New York: Warner Books, 1987), pp. 219–222. Miller and Heiman's research and ideas are discussed in greater detail in Chapter 5.

CHAPTER **3** **Building a Team**
Development Staffing for Libraries

The key to a successful library fundraising program is a synergistic relationship between development professionals and librarians. The ingredients of this partnership are a commitment to shared goals and an atmosphere of trust and respect that fosters a dynamic exchange of information and ideas between development people and library people. The library director sets the tone for this partnership and facilitates the relationship between librarians and development staff.

Unfortunately, for many library directors, the hiring of a professional development staff is not possible financially nor is it realistic in relation to the size of their organizations and the extent of their fundraising goals. If they are to raise money, library directors must play the roles of both mountain climber *and* Sherpa guide. This chapter specifically describes these roles in a way that will benefit even readers who do not have the luxury of a development team.

This chapter draws on the authors' examination and observation of library development programs around the country. Some of the development programs are successful, but many are not. The purpose of this chapter is to help you avoid the mistakes that are currently hurting development programs.

At the outset, the fundamental decision before you is, "What kind of development program should I have?" There are two paths from which to choose: (1) an ambitious fundraising program that concentrates on raising major gifts, a *major-gifts program,* and (2) a less ambitious, but perfectly respectable, program that concentrates on a Friends group, mail appeals, tie-ins to the university's annual fund and other interest groups, and middle-range givers, a path we call an *annual-giving program.* The program you choose should be based on both your personal aptitude for fundraising and the size and ambition of your library-fundraising goals.

STAFFING A MAJOR-GIFTS PROGRAM

It is worth noting again here that the library director is the head of the development staff and that his leadership is essential for any program that intends to seek major gifts. In Chapter 1, we discussed the need for the library director to commit a significant portion of her time to raising money if she elects a major-gifts program, and we noted that the implication of this was that she would need a strong executive team to free her from daily concerns over operational matters. Ideally, the library director will have a deputy for operations who attends to many of the day-to-day concerns of the library and oversees the library's associate directors. The director will delegate all but the most important matters to subordinates, who are given authority as well as responsibility to manage their areas.

If you elect to have a major-gifts program, you will need a development professional to handle the major-gifts fundraising effort. This position is usually referred to as a "director of development." The job of your director of development is to look after and expand the number of donors from whom 90 percent of your funding will come. A more detailed discussion of this person's role in the development program and what you can expect from him follows later in this chapter. Very ambitious library programs, ones involving multimillion-dollar capital campaigns, often have additional major-gifts staff.

You cannot expect your director of development to seek major gifts and to handle the support group. To do so is both unrealistic in terms of the development director's time and unjustifiable in terms of financial return, since Friends groups are so rarely sources of major gifts. If you already have a Friends group and you want to have a major-gifts program, but can only afford one position, think in terms of phasing in a second position for the Friends. Ambitious major-gifts programs will benefit immeasurably from having an additional person to manage the Friends and coordinate events. Friends groups and events consume vast amounts of time and can easily distract your development staff from its primary function, which is to raise money. This additional position is definitely worthwhile if you have an active program involving such things as regular Friends programs, frequent lunches and dinner parties, and other large-scale events such as black-tie galas. (Some universities operate a central events office that can be depended upon for some of these functions. If you are in a university, see what support this office can offer you and plan your staffing accordingly.) All of your development professionals will require clerical support—at a minimum, a shared clerical position with another department.

STAFFING AN ANNUAL-GIVING PROGRAM

A library development program that does not endeavor to seek major gifts, but opts instead for an annual-giving program, concentrates on a Friends group, mail appeals, middle-range givers, and, in a university setting, tie-ins to the annual fund and other interest groups. This type of program uses a Friends group to serve primarily a development purpose, with the other benefits of Friends groups—enhanced public relations, political advocacy, a source of volunteer labor—being considered valuable but secondary. We discuss the purpose and management of a Friends group in detail in Chapter 6. For now, suffice it to say that one way to ensure that a Friends group is an effective fundraising tool is to put a development professional in charge of it, as opposed to a librarian who has little or no fundraising experience. Asking your special collections librarian, for example, to be in charge of the Friends is, in most situations, anachronistic and unrealistic. It is far better to involve the head of special collections in cultivation and stewardship activities.

The management of a dynamic library Friends group can be a good opportunity for people pursuing a career in development, public relations, or marketing. It can be a challenging and rewarding proving ground in which they will get the opportunity to work with volunteers, plan events, apply public relations techniques, and produce publications. Clerical support may be necessary to support this position, and at least half of a position could be given to a writer/editor who can produce a Friends' newsletter, the library's journal (if there is one), and any other public-relations publications issued by the library.

SELECTING DEVELOPMENT STAFF

The library must find development professionals who are energetic, who can make intelligent choices about where to focus effort, who are capable of identifying prospects, and who can orchestrate a cultivation and solicitation strategy that will turn prospects into donors. For obvious reasons, these individuals need to have highly developed interpersonal skills. What is perhaps less obvious, they must also possess excellent writing skills, for a large portion of their work involves writing gift proposals and artfully subtle letters.[1]

Identifying and choosing good fundraisers can be difficult for librarians because fundraisers are completely different from the personnel they are used to hiring. Other specialists, such as programmers, have educational credentials that qualify them for their positions. Not so with fundraisers; there is no body of knowledge over which they can demonstrate mastery, nor can they provide evidence of mastery in the form of a degree.[2] Unlike librarians, few development people are active professionally; few fundraisers attend conferences, give talks, or subscribe to fundraising journals.

Beyond interpersonal skills and writing skills, what should a librarian look for when seeking to hire a fundraiser? Trying to find someone with a good track record is meaningless, since successful fundraising depends much more on the leader than on the fundraiser. Far more important than the fundraiser's track record is the library director's ability to work well with the fundraiser. In this relationship, *chemistry* is essential; it is even more important than experience. The librarian and the fundraiser must be able to work well as a team and come across well as a team. They should be able to relate to one another in a brainstorming mode; they should be able to establish an atmosphere of mutual trust, support, and respect. The librarian and the fundraiser must be able to enter into a *psychological contract:* each must have a regard for the other that extends beyond the boundaries of ordinary working relationships.

One solution to finding a fundraiser with whom you can establish a psychological contract is to look around your institution and at other institutions that are similar to yours and find out who the talented fundraisers are. Get to know them and see if there is any chemistry between you. When you find the right person (something you should recognize almost immediately), try to recruit her. But realize that the library will not be thought of as a glamorous fundraising assignment; on the contrary, it will most likely be thought of as difficult, even thankless. Most fundraisers want to associate themselves with programs that are likely to be winners and involve high stakes, such as those found in schools of law, medicine, or business. They want to be able to say, for purposes of their own advancement, that they participated in a successful $60 million campaign, for example. Libraries just are not in that league. Therefore, be prepared to make a good offer, including not only salary but also the best office you can provide and any other perks at your disposal.

Working with a Development Staff

As a library director, you can think of your relationship with your development officer as being like that of a mountain climber and a Sherpa guide, or you can think of yourself as the star and the fundraiser as the movie director. In either case, the development officer is your "moves manager." She arranges logistical matters, provides you with necessary information, and sets the scene for your development work. It may be appropriate for other people who work for you to defer to you, but this is not so with your development director. Very often, you will be in the position of taking direction from your fundraiser, who will say, "I need you to host this dinner, take this trip, and call these people and say these things to them."

For these reasons, there should never be organizational barriers between the development staff and the library director. When consultants or
other fundraisers see organizational distance between the director and the
development staff, they know the program is in trouble. If you as the
library director have your development staff report to someone below you,
it will be difficult for you to participate fully in the development effort, and
therefore your program has little chance of succeeding.[3]

Your development staff should help you identify and cultivate prospects,
identify linkages between volunteers and prospects, assess the potential of
prospects, and assist in writing proposals. They should supply prospect
leads and act as a liaison with other development staffs, such as, in a
university, the staff in the planned-giving office. The staff should do the
nitty-gritty advance work and the follow-up. They should show creativity in
coming up with ways to approach companies and foundations. They
should supply guidance. Above all, your development staff should help you
with strategy, especially with regard to the four elements of messages
described in Chapter 2 in connection with communication theory.

If you cannot afford a development staff, then you will have to do all of this
yourself. For some people this is possible, but their success will depend on the
amount of time they can devote solely to development. You will find that a
capable administrative assistant is a must, and that a colleague with whom
you can brainstorm and discuss donor strategy is invaluable.

Because, unfortunately, there are so many unrealistic expectations being placed on library development staff, it is revealing to ask the question,
"What should I *not* expect from my development staff?" You should not
expect your development staff to keep your librarians briefed on the
development effort. That is your job. You should not expect them to take
over the care and feeding of everyone who has ever made a gift; it is up to
the people who have established relationships with past donors to maintain those relationships. You should not ask your staff to look for a donor
for any project or need that comes along, and they should not be involved
with gifts of books; these should be handled by the gifts section or by the
appropriate librarian in consultation, if necessary, with the professional
fundraiser.

Though development shares certain features with public relations, do
not confuse the two. Producing press releases, annual reports, and merchandise such as note cards is not development. Finally, you must resist
the temptation to burden your major-gifts person with the planning of
frequent special events. Generally speaking, events are not a good fundraising technique. Unless they are underwritten, fundraising events usually raise very little money. General cultivation events might promote
goodwill, but they definitely do not raise money. The best advice is to be
extremely selective in this area, as we explain in Chapter 7.

In addition to not burdening your development staff with inappropriate tasks, you should not create or subject them to a hostile environment. Engaging in a we-versus-they relationship with the central development office of a university is one way of producing a hostile environment since your fundraiser is bound to be caught in the middle. The library staff may prove to be another source of hostility from which you will have to shield your development people. Some of the "implementers" and "analyzers" in your library may harbor resentments toward the development program and may disparage development as frivolous in contrast to their "real" work. This can be aggravated by an envy of the glamorous lives that fundraisers are sometimes assumed to lead. Furthermore, since fundraising results, like those of sales, are quantifiable, library staff are sometimes tempted to evaluate fundraising results solely on the basis of dollars raised and ignore the total value, some of it nonmonetary, that gifts bring to the library. Lastly, you must not allow any of your own misgivings about fundraising to manifest themselves in ways that might be harmful to your fundraising effort.

Just as hostility will impair your fundraising program, so will frustration. Your being frequently out-of-town or unavailable for meetings with donors is a sure way to frustrate your development staff. In general, inflexibility about scheduling is a serious hindrance to fundraising. Also, be careful not to paralyze your development staff by involving the wrong people in their activities. A committee of librarians should never be charged with tasks related to fundraising; it is highly unlikely that they will have the necessary understanding of the issues and processes of development. Trust your development professionals to work freely, for example, with graphic designers and public relations professionals on fundraising literature. These documents do not lend themselves to a collective approach.

Having found talented fundraisers with whom you are capable of having a psychological contract, you do not want to lose them. You are probably a lot more vulnerable to losing your fundraiser than you may realize. The average amount of time a fundraiser stays in a position is about two years. Experienced fundraisers are in demand and receive job offers. They also have contacts that they can turn into nonfundraising jobs, such as a management position in a business or foundation. If they see problems in the library program, they can and will bail out.[4]

When you lose a fundraiser, you lose the contacts, ideas, and relationships that she has built. It probably will take many months for you to recruit a new fundraiser; it can easily take a year for your new fundraiser to understand your organization and to begin to know your prospects. It may even take longer for him to be in a position to set up a successful solicitation. In fact, fundraising headhunters will tell you that it takes three to five years for a development director to make a mark.

If you lose a fundraiser, you will inevitably lose information. And if the fundraiser has been with you for a while, you will almost certainly lose prospects, too. In a worst-case scenario, you will have subsidized your fundraiser's education of the donor community and will have enabled her to establish relations that she can then take to her next position. She becomes more marketable as a fundraiser, while you are left starting from scratch. Another concern is that, if you lose a fundraiser, you run the risk of having your prospects "stolen" by other fundraisers in your institution. This danger is especially common in the university setting.

There is no comparable staffing analogy in libraries. When you lose a reference librarian, you can replace him, knowing that a new person will come already equipped to handle the essentials of the job. Not so with a fundraiser. Yes, the new person will know how to do the job, but, since the sources are people rather than standard reference books, and the people are specific to your institution, it will take time—a lot of time—for the development person to become productive.

Development Staffing for the Academic Library

The uniqueness and complexity of the university fundraising environment merit special comment. At colleges and universities, the library development effort operates within the context of a centralized development effort for the institution. University library development offices and central development offices use one of three different organizational relationships: (1) the development staff are hired by and paid by the library and function outside the realm of the central development office; (2) the development staff are hired and paid by the library, the central development office, or a combination of the two, and they report to both the library and the central development office; (3) the development staff are hired and paid by the central development office and are assigned to the library and possibly to other departments but report only to the central development office. In the first model, the development staff are entirely "library." In the second, there is a mixture of library and central development. In the third, the development staff assigned to the library "belong" strictly to central development.

Some form of the second option, the dual approach, is becoming the most common scenario.[5] Though dual reporting relationships are often difficult for the development staff, this arrangement offers definite advantages for the library. It is particularly advantageous to the library to be fully integrated into the systems and services of the central development office. Librarians should be aware of what these systems and services are and of the ways in which they can benefit the library's fundraising efforts. We will have more to say about this in the following section.

Under this dual arrangement, who pays for the salaries and budget of the development staff is a matter for negotiation between the library and the senior administration of the university. It is not unusual for central development to pay for the major-gifts staff and for the library to pay for the annual-fund staff. If the library has to pay for all of the salaries, is it worth it? Yes, because you will easily recover salaries and will likely bring in many times your expenditure, though perhaps not within the first fiscal year or even the second; it usually takes three to five years for a development program to bear fruit.

The library development operation also requires a budget, another matter for negotiation. Typically, development budgets include line items for cultivation activities (from lunches with individual donors to large events), recognition activities (such as installing plaques and publishing honor rolls), and other needs such as publications, stationery and postage, systems and data costs, and travel.

WORKING WITH THE CENTRAL DEVELOPMENT OFFICE

Typically, a university's development operation is part of a larger department of public affairs or university relations. Often this office will oversee, in addition to development, alumni relations, public relations, the university foundation, and the alumni and donor records system. Even seasoned information professionals like librarians might well be impressed by the scope of some of these systems. In size and complexity, the public affairs departments of universities may rival the library operation, employing hundreds of people and having multimillion-dollar budgets.

While many areas of universities, especially athletic departments, have had development operations for a long time, most libraries are relative newcomers to the scene. For this reason, and because libraries have no alumni to call their own, it can sometimes seem that all of the university's big donors are already committed to other areas—that all the good prospects are taken.

The best way of establishing links between the library and new prospects is to have the university's leader give a high priority to the library. The president is in a position to persuade key volunteers to redirect their interests. Conversely, nothing is quite so detrimental to library development as a president who is indifferent to the library's role and needs.

Another good technique is to cultivate interest in the library among members of the board of trustees. Membership on a university's board of trustees, it is understood, commits its members to support the university with substantial gifts of their own and to help find new supporters by using their clout and drawing on their contacts in the community. "Give, get, or get off," is a phrase used in this context. Trustees can often be helpful in suggesting names of people who might become donors to the library. Since the central development office manages the board, senior members of the development staff broker access to them. This situation is another indication of the importance of maintaining good relations with your university's central development office.

All university development offices employ a clearance system of one kind or another to ensure that prospects are not bombarded with solicitations from different areas of the institution. Hence, solicitations—and, for that matter, even simple contacts with prospects—can require prior clearance of some kind from the central development staff. Obtaining these clearances is the responsibility of your development officer.

Your development officer will likely report to one member of the senior development staff, and this person will frequently be in the position of denying you access to the prospects whom you would most like to see. In fact, it may seem that this person's role has more to do with vetoing ideas than anything else. What, then, should this senior development staff member be contributing to the development effort? In the interests of equity, with every veto should come an alternative. The senior development person is, at least in theory, in that position by virtue of having a sense of the big development picture; he should be contributing new ideas and contacts constantly. It is a good idea to get this expectation out in the open early in your relationship to avoid disappointment later on.

The central development office maintains several systems and services that can be useful to the library development program. Most development offices use the services of consultants, for example. From time to time you might find it useful to ask a fundraising consultant to assess your program, especially if you have a problem with your program but see that, politically, it would be better to have someone other than you point it out. Most central development offices also employ several full-time writers whose job it is to prepare campaign materials and proposals for donors. In addition, the research department will provide profiles on donor prospects that will help to determine prospects' giving capabilities and give a more complete picture of their background.

Virtually all universities maintain a data base that tracks alumni, donors, and sometimes prospects. The office in the university that manages this data base can produce customized donor lists, such as lists of all cash donors to the library within a given time frame, or one organized in dollar-descending order.

These data bases can be useful in other ways, too. For example, you might meet someone at a Friends event whom you do not know and from whom you have little chance to obtain information. Having learned the person's name, however, you should be able to ask your development officer to run a check against the university's data base. Such a check will reveal if the person or any of the person's immediate family have degrees from the university and if they have any history of giving to the university. It will also reveal the person's address, which is frequently an indicator of means.

Some universities use proprietary programs called "electronic screening" that analyze their local alumni/donor data bases to assess giving potential. These programs, modeled on systems devised by the consumer marketing industry for targeting direct-mail advertising, assign codes to individual donor records that represent certain life-style characteristics based on the donor's home address and, sometimes, other public information.

We cannot leave the subject of working with the central development office without addressing the touchy subject of collegial relations. Unfortunately, relations between the library and the central development office can all too easily become adversarial. If negotiating over salaries and the reporting structure does not create hostilities, there will be innumerable other opportunities for breeding ill will. Librarians often become upset when they are unable to obtain clearance from the central development office to approach certain prospects. For its part, the development office abhors what it sometimes sees as the library's halfhearted efforts, shifting priorities, and inflexibility on the subject of gift opportunities and recognition. If efforts to raise money falter, each side may blame the other. In some cases, the relationship can deteriorate to the point that drastic measures, including the removal of staff on both sides, become necessary.

To work together successfully, the library and the central development office must agree on and abide by a set of ground rules and strive to maintain a respectful and productive working relationship. The central development office requires the following from the library director: a substantial commitment of time to the fundraising effort, agreement to clear all major-gift prospects through the central office, unambiguous and firm priorities, and realistic expectations about gift opportunities. The library requires of the central development office: an effort to provide access to top prospects, ideas about new prospects and access to them, and access to the president of the university and top volunteers such as trustees when appropriate.

The library stands to gain a great deal by cooperating with the central development office since senior development staff are in a position to influence the assignment of unrestricted gifts or direct a donor toward the library. If your library develops a poor reputation with the development office, these important benefits will be lost, with potentially damaging consequences to your program. Do not underestimate the extent to which the development office can open the way to a multitude of opportunities.

LIBRARY STAFF MEMBERS AND DEVELOPMENT

The success of your development program can be greatly enhanced if, in addition to the library director, other librarians contribute to the effort. Earlier we said that development officers are like Sherpa guides, while library directors, with their leadership and vision, are like mountain climbers. When other librarians participate in the development effort, they sometimes play the role of the Sherpa guide and other times that of the mountain climber. For example, a librarian acts as a Sherpa guide when the library director or the development officer asks her to supply information about a donor or project in preparation for a meeting or proposal. In such cases, librarians lend Sherpa-like assistance to the behind-the-scenes development work. In other cases, librarians act as mountain climbers when they use their positional clout, just as the library director does, to obtain a gift. In these situations, librarians are out in front, interacting with potential donors and building relationships with them, and they are supported by the development officer, who makes meeting arrangements, writes follow-up letters, initiates research on the individuals, and attends to any other necessary tasks.

Every library has people who are natural mountain climbers, and these people can make an enormous difference to the success of your fundraising program. (Your development director usually recognizes these people almost immediately.) Mountain climbers are especially effective, of course, when they are in certain key positions, such as the headship of special collections or the associate directorship for collection development. When possible, add these mountain climbers on your library staff to the development team.

Being added to the team means that they attend weekly meetings with the development staff and the library director and actively serve the development effort by identifying and cultivating prospects and discussing gifts with them. Just as in mountaineering, the more able people you have climbing, the higher the peaks you can surmount. Knowing this, you may be tempted to add people to the team who are not really mountain climbers, but who you hope might potentially contribute to the team. This is a natural impulse but, unfortunately, not realistic in most cases. *Your mountain climbers will be obvious to you.*

To extend the mountain-climbing metaphor, it is also possible to trigger avalanches that slow you down and injure your team. Throughout this book we alert you to possible avalanches; the chart shows some of the most common of these. Of all the possible avalanches, the greatest and most damaging is the "executive sign off on development issues" avalanche. In this scenario, the library director brings development matters before the executive group, who often will bury them under a mountain of objections. *You will never get far from base camp if you take develop-ment matters before the executive group.* This is not to suggest that you should not communicate with the executive group about development matters, but development only succeeds if you free it from the traditional constraints of library management, and, unfortunately, associate directors often tend to try to control or subvert development efforts that they see as frivolous or as an easy target in budget and power struggles. Having little or no experience with fundraising, they may be tempted to straitjacket a process that requires flexibility. It is useful to remember that development, like leadership, is ultimately *your* responsibility.

Nine Ways to Trigger Avalanches

1. Have the executive group sign off on development issues.
2. Emphasize a lot of little donors rather than a few big ones.
3. Don't support development staff or, even better, subject them to hostility.
4. Refuse to decide on your priorities or, once you do, change them often.
5. Ask for "needs assessments" and "case statements."
6. Mistake public relations for development.
7. Rely on volunteers to do fundraising for you.
8. Overemphasize governmental grants.
9. Avoid or neglect fundraising; create a latch-key development program.

THE DEVELOPMENT TEAM AND THE FUNDRAISING SWIMMING POOL

To visualize how the library development team works together to coordinate the development process, let's leave mountains and avalanches and return to an earlier metaphor, the fundraising swimming pool. Picture a swimming pool staffed by your development team. Your annual-fund person is down in the shallow end. He is in part a social director, structuring activities for everyone who might get into the pool by joining the Friends, making some other small gift, or by otherwise showing interest in being involved with the library devel-opment effort. The annual-fund person is especially alert to anyone in the shallow end who might be able to swim to the deep end. Upon identifying such an individual, the annual-fund person will encourage her to venture into the deeper waters, perhaps by introducing her to the library director, and will alert the rest of the development team to this fact.

Meanwhile, the major-gifts person is attending to the deep end. She has been involved in setting up private pool-side chats between the library director and major-gift prospects. Sometimes she will use a Friends event as a cultivation opportunity before the prospect has made a gift, but such an event is never used as a substitute for one-to-one cultivation, only as an augmentation to it. Once a gift has been made, the major-gifts person serves as a kind of lifeguard, seeing to it that the donors become honorary Friends members and that they enjoy their experience in the pool. One way she does this is by unfailingly checking RSVP lists for Friends events and then alerting the library director and other members of the development team when a major donor is expected to come to an event. This way they can plan who needs to say what to whom. What they will say usually involves renewed expressions of thanks, an update on the gift, and remarks that will pave the way for resolicitation.

The more people you have in your library who are good at swimming in, or overseeing, the fundraising pool, the better. The library director, the head of special collections, the associate director for collection development, and the gifts librarian all potentially act as rovers by socializing with people at both ends of the pool, helping to assure that the entire experience is pleasurable. More important, these additional members of your fundraising team can be productive pool-side, too, by recruiting both annual givers and major givers. Few prospects will seek out fundraisers; usually, prospects prefer to talk to the library director, the head of special collections, or some other appropriate member of the library staff. This is why you need the dynamic people in your library assisting you in the important task of bringing new people into your pool of donors.

Development is about people—the people who give, namely your donors, and the people who help you get, namely your development team. Now, how do you tailor your program to take advantage of your personal and organizational strengths? This question is addressed in the next chapter.

NOTES

1. A persuasive case can be made for hiring fundraisers with a public relations/communication background. Public relations professionals tend to be good writers and understand communication with external groups. Kelly has gone so far as to argue that, theoretically, the fundraising function should be subordinate to the public relations function. See Kathleen S. Kelly, *Fund Raising and Public Relations: A Critical Analysis* (Hillsdale, N.J.: Lawrence Erlbaum, 1991), passim.

2. Indiana University's Center for Philanthropy is developing a five-course certificate program for fundraisers that will be the only one of its kind in the country. The nearest thing to an existing credential in the fundraising profession is the Certified Fund Raising Executive (C.F.R.E.), which is granted by the National

Society of Fund Raising Executives after successful completion of a one-day written exam and proof of five years' experience in the profession. Relative to the number of fundraisers in the country, only a small number have the C.F.R.E. It would not be unusual for there to be no one with the C.F.R.E. in a large university development operation.

3. Physical distance between the library director and the development staff can be an indicator of problems, too. If possible, the development staff should be based in the director's suite.

4. See Kelly, p. 495. Kelly describes fundraisers as "lay administrators who are highly paid, in great demand, change jobs frequently, are generally young, and are often inexperienced."

5. Association of Research Libraries, Office of Management Services. *Library Development and Fund Raising Capabilities*, OMS Systems and Procedures Exchange Center, SPEC Kit 146 (Washington, D.C.: ARL, OMS, July/August 1988), pp. 6–7 and cf. the May 1983 *SPEC Kit on Fundraising* #94.

4 **Planning to Raise Funds**
Understanding, Initiating, and Evaluating
Your Development Program

In the first three chapters we covered some basic issues: the importance of assessing your personal qualities and outlook as they relate to fundraising, the need to understand some basic concepts of fundraising, and the factors to consider when building a development team. Now we can turn to the practical issues of creating and implementing your fundraising program. As you begin your program, it may be tempting to look around and ask first, "How do other people do it?" and perhaps to add, "We need a plan." Resist this temptation. Before you begin the planning process and before you try other people's methods or those you have had success with in the past, think about what you are going to plan and why you are planning it. Ask instead, "What are we trying to do?" and, "Why *are* we doing what we're doing?" Instead of looking at what others are doing, first ask, "How are we different from everyone else?" (e.g., from other libraries, universities, or nonprofit organizations) and, "What is the fundraising environment like in my particular institution?"

In this chapter we describe a process that involves understanding your library's purposes and uniqueness, identifying its niche, utilizing a strategic plan, beginning your fundraising program, and evaluating its effectiveness.[1] The goal of this chapter is not to prescribe a planning method, but to guide you in *how to think* about the purpose and role of planning in library development. Such an understanding will help you to avoid both the mistake of planning for the sake of planning and the trap of naively adopting fundraising practices that may have worked in other places but will not necessarily work in yours.

FINDING YOUR NICHE

Where your library's purposes and uniqueness converge is its special niche (see figure 3). Before you start planning your fundraising program, it

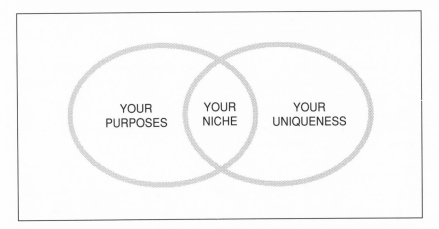

Figure 3. Finding your niche

is critical that you understand your library's niche. To arrive at this point, first think about your library's purpose. Ask yourself a fundamental question that you may not have considered in a long time: "Why are we doing what we're doing? Why *are* we running this library?" Initially, the answers may seem obvious to you, but, if you examine the question seriously, the exercise may be valuable in rekindling your enthusiasm for your job. It may provide you with a renewed appreciation of how your organization benefits its various constituencies and help you reawaken the basic assumptions and beliefs that are the key to articulating your vision with freshness and excitement. Most important in terms of fundraising, the answers that you come up with may supply you with those very ideas that will attract, stimulate, and motivate donors.

Once you have clarified your sense of purpose in running your library, you should consider the purpose of having a library development program. Bear in mind that a development program should exist to promote the growth and enhancement of first-rate libraries. It should exist to bridge the gap between mediocrity and excellence or to make what is already excellent better still: to go from where you are to where you aspire to be.

Define your aspirations in terms of definite, forward-looking goals. By forward-looking goals, we mean positive projects that advance the library. Do not conceive of your development program as a deficit-closing mechanism. Your neediness will not motivate donors.

In addition to clarifying your goals and purposes, it is also essential to consider how your library is different from every other, how it is unique. Everything about your library contributes to its own special character. Your building, your publications, your history, your traditions, your collections, your programs, and everyone who works, or has worked, in your library are all unique to it. Your library's environment is also crucial: your physical setting, your parent organization, your city, your geographic base, your economic base—all these contribute to its character, too.

The library of a large public research university is very different from the library of a small, private liberal arts college. A medium-sized public library in suburban Connecticut differs from a large public library in Los Angeles. One should not aspire to be like the other, either operationally or in its approach to fundraising. Fundraising is a relatively unexplored field. It is legitimate for you to invent your own program and test your own ideas.[2]

An appreciation of the concept of uniqueness is also valuable in your relations with donors. Just as you and your library are unique, so each major donor prospect is unique. Every relationship with a potential major donor has a singular quality and character. Donors do not want to be treated impersonally; they want to be appreciated for who they are.

To understand your niche, return to your purposes and uniqueness and think about where they converge. Step back and look at your traditional and emerging strengths, examine the population you serve, the economic base of your region, how your location has an impact on your identity and circumstances, and who you know—to mention just a few of the areas you might think about. You might also try to imagine how a colleague at another library would characterize your library.

Understanding your niche will help you to clarify your priorities; concentrating on just one or two priorities will give you focus in working with donors and in articulating your achievements and future goals in your publications and in your gift proposals. Understanding your niche helps you to do the right thing, too, especially when it comes to evaluating the acceptance of money or collections when they are offered with strings attached. At various points, that is, you will likely be approached by potential donors who will offer to provide money for specific, specialized purposes if certain conditions are met. For example, a donor may offer to give you a large and valuable collection in a particular field and also promise substantial annual support if you will commit space and staff to run the operation. The questions then become, "Will this fit in our niche? Is this consonant with our identity? Is there instruction or research being done in this subject at our institution? What are the financial trade-offs involved in committing staff time to the operation? Would these positions have to be funded at the expense of more critical needs? Are we looking at an opportunity or a boondoggle?"

"Selective excellence" is a phrase being used more and more on university campuses. Selective excellence involves a university's assessment of its purposes and uniqueness and its strengths and weaknesses. Few schools can devote a high level of resources to all academic areas. Keeping an academic library's identity in line with the university's priorities is becoming more important than ever financially, politically, and academically. In the sometimes freewheeling, high-stakes world of development, it is important to maintain a clear vision of how the library's niche should complement the university's selective excellence, or niche, so to speak. This may sound simple, but it will not be so simple in practice. As a library leader, your commitment to your niche will be tested frequently as individual donors and pressure groups urge that their visions be adopted.

In the public library setting, this concept of niche is in large part captured through the formal planning exercise known as role setting, inasmuch as the process determines a role that responds to community needs and assesses the capacity of the library to meet them. Whatever terms are used, the planning process should result in a library development program that contributes to the independence, or autonomy, of the library and that supports, to the greatest extent possible, the vision and priorities of the library. Martin Kramer put this matter well when he said that leaders should be both entrepreneurial and protective.[3] You will be entrepreneurial in setting out your vision and seeking financial support but protective of your library's well-being by understanding, and constantly keeping in view, your particular niche.

FUNDRAISING PLANNING METHODS

Be conservative about how much information you gather in the process of arriving at an understanding of purposes and uniqueness and in your planning process. Avoid gathering information before you know the purpose of the information. Rather than gather useless data, the first thing to do is to acquire an appreciation of your environment. Who are the "players"? Who, that is, are your best prospects? What opportunities are there for them to help and be involved in a significant way?

Many commonly used methods of beginning a development effort are ineffective and frustrating precisely because they violate this principle of limited information gathering. Too often, libraries begin a fundraising effort by conducting a needs assessment. Since your fundraising program can only focus on two or three priorities, a survey of all of your library's needs is a waste of time and obscures your statement of development priorities. Even worse, you may create false expectations. If you canvass widely for needs throughout your institution, you will probably receive suggestions and pleas from many parties. Once you prioritize the needs, those whose programs end up low on the list may become resentful.

Another poor method of beginning a fundraising effort is to ask the fundraiser to complete a comprehensive financial statement showing all of the library's past and current sources of income. The generation of such reports is not a fundraising function but an accounting exercise. New money does not magically result from counting dollars already received. Often such exercises are only futile efforts to infuse an appearance of rigor and some hardness into an unrigorous and soft process.

Another commonly misused method of beginning a fundraising effort is the case statement, which many fundraisers believe you must produce as virtually your first fundraising act. Traditionally, a case statement is a document, written by development officers in cooperation with the institution's various administrators, that attempts to make the case for private support in a succinct and compelling manner. It is usually printed in the form of an elegant brochure to be read by potential supporters.[4] Many fundraisers see the necessity of a case statement as unquestionable. They believe that you simply cannot raise money without one.[5] Having participated in a $55 million library capital campaign *without a case statement,* we disagree.

Though case statements are widely used, they have several serious conceptual flaws. The first problem with them is that the writing of the case statement is often spearheaded by the professional fundraiser. Though the development officer is not the leader of the organization—or even, for that matter, the leader of the fundraising program—he is expected to bring together the institution's various stakeholders, get them to agree on a vision, purpose, and priorities, and then translate that agreement into a publishable document for use with volunteers. Little wonder, then, that many fundraisers spend months, even years, on case statements that, if they are ever completed, are practically meaningless. The second major problem with case statements concerns the choice of the best message channel to communicate the message, an issue we discussed in Chapter 2. As we pointed out, library leaders and fundraisers should be communicating their case to their best prospects face-to-face, so why would they need an expensive, difficult-to-write printed piece? They don't. This is why many thousands of printed case statements sit in their unopened cartons in development-office storage rooms throughout the country.

A Better Method: Strategic Plans

Once you have arrived at an understanding of your purposes, uniqueness, niche, and priorities, you are ready to complete the planning process. Rather than squandering time and money to create a long list of needs, a rigorous but distracting financial statement, or an all-purpose case statement, create a solid strategic plan that your fundraiser is involved in developing, along with the library's other key constituent groups. A strategic plan is a highly specific, internal document generated by the leadership of an institution (not the fundraiser) that analyzes the program and outlines its future direction. When applied to development, a strategic plan becomes a launching pad for your fundraising program. Think of a strategic plan as an internal case statement that can be a source of recyclable boilerplate to be used in individual proposals and specific publications.

Much development work relies on the groundwork that has been laid in the form of strategic plans. Since strategic planning articulates where you are currently and where you aspire to be in the future, it provides the rationale for your development program. Because strategic planning also involves key constituencies in the examination process, it is a way of reconciling library fundraising opportunities with the priorities of the parent institution. Good strategic planning also balances the priorities of competing constituencies, be they within the prospect pool or within the organization. By using strategic planning in this way, skilled leaders set priorities without alienating those who have special interests.

Sometimes case statements are confused with strategic plans, and fundraisers try to use them to accomplish the goals of strategic planning. Many fundraisers have used the process of producing a case statement to involve constituencies and to get them to agree on fundraising priorities and fundraising goals. They have also found the process useful in building relationships, both internally and externally. All of these activities are vital to successful fundraising. It is essential that the fundraiser interact with the library's constituencies on these matters. However, these activities should be part of the strategic planning process, not an activity that is driven by the need for a fundraising document for external audiences.

Other Kinds of Plans

Sometimes you may need to produce development plans for the library's parent organization, which may require that you submit such documents as five-year plans. You should be able to produce such a document without undue difficulty if you have as a beginning your strategic plan for the library. Your five-year plan might take the form of a spreadsheet with a brief narrative. As you prepare such plans, remember the importance of having only two or three priorities; remember, too, the unpredictable nature of development.

Your development staff will likely be required to submit development plans to your parent organization, usually annually. These plans often include a list of prospects, cultivation strategies for them, and anticipated dollar results. Sometimes they include "gift tables" showing how many prospects are needed at various levels to reach a particular dollar goal. These plans generally require a fair amount of specificity about cash goals, the names of people who will be solicited, and a precise timetable for accomplishing this. In our opinion, this approach is another attempt to infuse hardness into a soft process. Good development is not done by formula. Therefore, these kinds of plans should be thought of as exercises only. Expecting much more from them is expecting your fundraiser to be a fortune teller.

Sometimes by "plans" fundraisers are referring to the infrastructures to support fundraising: prospect tracking systems, a system for acknowledging gifts, a way of handling gift accounting, and a method for monitoring stewardship activities. These infrastructures tend not to be as high a priority as they should be with fundraisers, who are generally evaluated by the bottom line. However, it is easy to see how weak infrastructures can harm your development program, directly affecting the bottom line. One internal system you should definitely review and improve, if necessary, is the library's gift accounting. You and your development staff will have frequent occasion to request information from your accounting staff. Be certain that the information-keeping runs smoothly.

A final word about plans: understand and remember the purposes of planning before producing any documents. Be sure there is a need or demand for them. Avoid planning for the sake of planning, and, above all, do not hide behind planning. Studies of university fundraising have shown that formal written plans are not strong indicators of fundraising success.[6] The real work of development is face-to-face contact with individuals; this is what you should give your attention to.

GETTING STARTED

If you have a clear understanding of your niche, a strategic plan for your library, and a list of viable prospects that you can begin to match up with your gift opportunities, you can get started on your development program. First, identify people you know who have MAGIC (means, age, givers, involvement, contacts). Once you have some names to work with, sit down with your development team and discuss strategy, name by name. This process is the heart of development, and you will be amazed at the creative ideas and bold plans that come out of such sessions. For example, say you went to school with someone who is now a wealthy and prominent member of your community. You have stayed in touch, and you happen to know that the person has a deep interest in some field of study, such as art history. It would seem natural to assume that this person might be interested in establishing an endowment, perhaps for the development of the art history collection (assuming that building your endowment is one of your priorities). In such cases the only caution is to avoid too narrowly defining your development opportunities in hopes of enticing someone to make a gift. Though totally unrestricted gifts are rare, many donors under-stand the importance of librarians having flexibility in spending decisions. In this example, it might be possible to interest the donor in supporting endowment for the collection without specifying a particular field.

Second, make contact with the prospect; you might call and ask to have lunch. Fill her in on your priorities, fundraising and otherwise, and ask her advice about something if you can. From there, invite her to some events, and so on. Find a role for her to play, such as membership on your Friends' board or visiting committee. Throughout these early stages of cultivation, the prospect will hear the fundraising message regularly, but in a non-threatening way. (In the next chapter, we describe specifically how to handle the later stages of cultivation and solicitation.)

If you feel you are short of viable prospects, building a list of such prospects will be your initial goal. Talk to the people you *do* know, and ask them for advice on meeting people who might have reason to be interested in your library. Seek ideas from people in your library and your develop-ment office. Think of faculty or other users who are well-connected and who might help open some doors for you. Then follow up on these leads.

Another good way to get started is to get to know other successful fundraisers in your organization, such as, in a university setting, the dean of the business school, law school, or other successful school or program. Ask them how they got started in fundraising and if they will share some of the fruits of their experience with you. Attend events sponsored by the central development office and watch your counterparts in action. In a very real way, getting started in development means adopting an attitude of interest and a commitment to doing it. It means looking at everything you do through the lens of development.

To take one example, suppose you have just been appointed library director. Your newness is not a liability, but an asset. It gives you a golden opportunity to launch your development effort. It allows you to call people and say, "I am the new director of such-and-such library, and I would like to meet you." Your new position gives you a reason to ask people to help you meet other people. It allows your development staff to work with you on developing a message about your priorities that you can communicate at public events aimed at your various constituencies (e.g., Friends, pros-pects, your staff, and your organization).

View everything that happens in your library as providing an opportu-nity to do development. Even potentially bad occurrences are opportuni-ties for relationship-building. Floods, fires, earthquakes, thefts, bad press, or other setbacks can all provide opportunities for you to communicate with your donors and major prospects. Call or visit them to say, "As one of the library's insiders, it is important that you hear about this occurrence from me. May I come and see you to tell you about it?" It is very important to treat your donors and prospects as insiders and to be constantly on the lookout for ways of communicating this. After you have built a relationship with a prospect, the next step is to ask for the gift, the subject of the next chapter.

The following list summarizes the steps in beginning your fundraising program.

Getting Started

1. Understand your purposes and uniqueness; know your niche.
2. Have a strategic plan.
3. Be sure your development staff has the necessary infrastructures in place.
4. Identify prospects with MAGIC and begin to match them up, if only loosely at first, with existing priorities.
5. One by one, develop cultivation strategies for your prospects and follow up on them.

EVALUATING YOUR PROGRAM

In the early stages of your program, think about the criteria by which you will evaluate it at some point in the future. What constitutes successful fundraising? Given the increasing pressure on libraries to raise funds, and the time and expense involved in development programs, it is important to be able to answer this question. Being aware of how you will define success will enable you to evaluate, analyze, and refine your program to ensure its effectiveness. This exercise will also be useful in defending your program—if that should become necessary—from detractors who do not understand or appreciate it.

Charitable organizations use a number of methods to determine the success of their fundraising efforts. Most of them measure success by the increase in dollars raised over the previous year. Also common are various kinds of cost-benefit analyses (dollars raised in relation to institutional expenditures) or dollars raised at one's own institution compared to those raised in a similar time period by a peer institution. The time period under consideration is usually one year.[7] The problem with these measures is that they use as their unit of analysis *only* dollars raised, neither taking into account external factors that affect fundraising totals nor addressing what we have already identified as the goal of development: *enhancing the organization's independence.*

There are a number of external factors that affect fundraising success which are not accounted for by measurements based solely on per-annum dollars raised. The fundraising program in a given year may not result in the receipt of a gift; yet the program may have, in that year, prepared the way for a gift that will be received in the future. The larger and more complex the gift, the more this is true. Also, forces beyond the control of fundraisers have a great impact on giving. Institutional characteristics (such as size, wealth, and prestige) and environmental factors (such as a scandal in the financial office of a university) dramatically affect gift income. Even broader factors, such as the state of the national economy, sometime affect giving.

But the most serious drawback to measuring fundraising effectiveness only by dollars raised per annum is that it rewards the indiscriminate seeking and acceptance of gifts and ignores the extent to which gifts contribute to the strategic vision, goals, and priorities of the organization.

It is likely that the institution you work for measures fundraising effectiveness on the basis of per-annum dollars raised. While recognizing that we must all be realistic about the status quo, we would encourage you to go a step further and evaluate the effectiveness of your library's fundraising program based on dollar totals *and gift utility*, and do this within a three- to five-year time frame rather than a one-year time frame. A gift's utility is measured by the extent to which it enables an organization to accomplish its objectives in support of organizational goals.[8]

Usually, unrestricted gifts have the highest value to your organization because their expenditure is left to your discretion. (Unfortunately, such gifts are rare.) Gifts in support of both current and previously established goals are of high value, as are budget-relief gifts that are designated for purposes already factored into your budget, thus allowing for the expenditure of budgeted funds in some other important area. Lowest in value are those gifts that do not align with the organization's goals and that may even cost more to accept than they are worth monetarily.

The concept of gift utility for libraries recognizes that fundraising is effective not when it reaps ever-increasing dollar amounts, but when gifts are in support of the library's goals and when the fundraising effort manages communication with donors and other key constituencies in a way that maintains the library's independence to the greatest extent possible. A true test of library fundraising effectiveness, therefore, might address the following three questions:

1. To what extent did gifts enhance or limit the independence of the library to pursue its established goals?
2. To what extent did gifts to the library satisfy the objectives of donors?

3. To what extent did gifts help the library fulfill the expectations of key constituencies other than donors?

Following Kelly, we recommend three ways these questions might be framed in evaluating your program.

1. *Evaluate fundraising based on dollar totals and gift utility.* Gifts to the library can be "weighted" on the basis of their contribution to established organizational goals (as opposed to fundraising dollar goals). Under such a system, a gift to a university library of $100,000 that could be used to advance the library's established programs would be worth more than the gift of a collection valued at $1 million in an area of marginal academic interest which would involve processing and space costs.

2. *Adopt an evaluation time frame longer than one year.* Annual assessments do not take into account the long-term nature of the fundraising process; a three- to five-year time frame is far better.

3. *Evaluate the process of fundraising in addition to the outcome.* In valuing the process of fundraising you recognize the quality and frequency of contacts with a potential donor. The aim is to deepen the person's relationship with your institution and to build his commitment to it incrementally. This does not mean, however, that the absence of conflict, either internally or externally, is a legitimate indicator of a successful development program. Since fundraising cannot be systematized as other aspects of the library can, it sometimes brings you into situations that offer the potential for conflict. In fact, as you reach across boundaries to establish relationships with prospects outside your organization, the level of conflict in your organization is likely to increase, at least for a time. This is not necessarily a bad thing. Conflict can stimulate positive change if properly managed to ensure the building of mutual understanding with donors and as much autonomy as possible for the library.

In ascribing to the principle of enhancing the library's independence, it is possible to move beyond simplistic methods of evaluation to a truer assessment of your program's effectiveness. Moreover, this approach will produce the kinds of quality relationships that do eventually result in large gifts.

In coming to the end of this chapter, we have reached a point where we can summarize the major indicators of a successful development program as well as those dangers to be avoided.

Positive Development Program Indicators

- The director provides visionary leadership.
- The director is the primary "driver" of the development program.
- The director understands the library's uniqueness and can communicate it with freshness and enthusiasm.
- The director sets two or three unwavering development priorities.
- The director understands his or her role as the tone setter for the library and shapes the library's image.
- A strategic plan is the foundation for the development program.
- There is a positive climate and working environment.
- The library has close relationships with community, donors, and the parent organization.
- The institution sees the library as a high priority.
- The director is willing to spend money to make money.
- The library director and the development professional have a psychological contract with one another.
- Development issues are not brought before the executive committee or other library committees but are the province of the director and the development staff.
- The development team focuses on the best prospects.
- The development team is committed to building incremental commitment and avoids formula fundraising.
- Fundraising is judged to be successful not primarily on the basis of dollars raised but to the extent that gifts contribute to the strategic vision of the library.
- The quality of contacts with potential donors is valued as much or more than the end result.

Development Program Danger Signals

- The director avoids or neglects development, creating a latch-key development program.
- Development staff don't stay.
- There are few donors.
- The program is directed to a long list of needs, instead of two or three priorities.
- Development matters are delayed or obstructed by the executive group.
- More attention is paid to broadening the base of donors than to cultivating a small group of large donors.
- The bottom line is all that matters.

NOTES

1. Many of the key ideas in this chapter are derived from Gerald Nadler and Shozo Hibino's invaluable *Breakthrough Thinking: Why We Must Change the Way We Solve Problems and the Seven Principles to Achieve This* (Rocklin, Calif.: Prima Publications & Communications, 1990).

2. Research on this matter bears out our own observation and experience that successful development programs often defy traditional fundraising practices. See Margaret A. Duronio and Bruce A. Loessin, *Effective Fund Raising in Higher Education* (San Francisco: Jossey-Bass, 1991). Their work has shown that universities that raise more money than their peer institutions do so because they do not follow the conventional wisdom in fundraising.

3. Martin Kramer, *The Venture Capital of Higher Education: The Private and Public Sources of Discretionary Funds* (San Francisco: The Carnegie Foundation for the Advancement of Teaching, 1980), p. 10.

4. See Harold Seymour, *Designs for Fund-Raising* (New York: McGraw-Hill, 1966), pp. 42–47, for the traditional view of the functions of a case statement. For an example of an actual case statement, see Francis C. Pray, ed., *Handbook for Educational Fund Raising* (San Francisco: Jossey-Bass, 1981), pp. 413–418.

5. To cite just one of many possible examples: Donald A. Miltner, "The Case Statement," in *Funding Alternatives for Libraries,* eds., Patricia Senn Breivik and E. Burr Gibson, (Chicago: American Library Association, 1979), p. 33. Lately, however, some observers have begun to question the value of case statements. For example, Dwight Burlingame writes, "Certainly, most donors do not give because of campaign literature. In fact, flashy literature can be a turn off." Though he goes on to say that campaign literature is important in telling your story, he concludes, "For major gifts, a tailor-made proposal is a must." "Library Capital Campaigns," in *Library Development: A Future Imperative,* ed. Dwight Burlingame, (New York: Haworth Press, 1990), pp. 97–98. And Patricia Forsythe writes, "In preparing the case statement, perhaps too much energy and money were expended for too little impact. . . . It has been my observation that people become obsessed with their case statements. . . . It will not do the fund raising for your organization." "An Endowment Campaign for a Public Library," in *Library Development,* ed. Dwight Burlingame, p. 109.

6. See Duronio and Loessin, p. 217.

7. This section draws on Kathleen S. Kelly, *Fund Raising and Public Relations: A Critical Analysis* (Hillsdale, N.J.: Lawrence Erlbaum, 1991), especially Chapter 14.

8. For a discussion of the concept of gift utility, see Kelly, p. 440.

5 ## Getting to Yes

The Major-Gifts Process

Most of your gifts will come from just a few major givers, but these gifts will account for as much as 90 percent of the money you raise. In light of this fact, major gifts should be the heart of your fundraising program. This chapter gives you specific guidance on handling the later stages of the development cycle—mature cultivation followed by solicitation. But, as we have repeatedly emphasized, "scoring" a gift is not the ultimate goal of fundraising. Reaching a win-win outcome for both donor and recipient is.

Ethical fundraising seeks mutual satisfaction for all parties. Following a successful solicitation, both giver and receiver should believe that their best interests have been served. The prospect is not an adversary, not a quarry or prey who must be trapped, cornered, or captured. There should be no coercion, trickery, or manipulation in approaching, asking, or completing a major-gift solicitation. The development process proceeds from an ethical base, leaving no room for a "whatever works" approach. After the gift is made, all commitments to donors must be fulfilled, or, if changing circumstances require alterations of commitments, these must be renegotiated openly.

Beware of development advice that encourages brazen and simple-minded sales techniques. Much misguided thinking about cultivation and solicitation is derived from sales concepts that are themselves outmoded and that were never in any case suitable to library fundraising. For example, salespeople used to think that the more customers they gave their pitch to, the greater their ultimate return would be. According to this approach, success was simply a numbers game. Another technique, called "track selling," operated on the idea that a salesperson should stick to a game plan, opening with a friendly or zippy grabber and proceeding through a script to one of several set closes. Track selling leads to the belief that the more cleverly developed your technique, the better able you are to "push" a product. It also leads to such simple-minded and mechanical notions as "plan the work and work the plan."[1] Because these old-fashioned sales techniques are one sided, and therefore at odds with the two-way, win-win outcome we advocate, we prefer to avoid altogether language that smacks of sales (e.g., "selling" gift opportunities, "closing" the deal).

Today's enlightened salespeople have moved beyond these approaches. They have come to see that people buy for their own reasons, not for the seller's. They understand that people do not buy a product merely for the product itself but for what it will do for them. Every customer has a mind-set that is personal and unique and that is linked to the individual's values, needs, and attitudes. Sophisticated salesmanship no longer depends on the sales pitch, but on the customer and his mind-set. Even the sales business has, in other words, moved to more of a two-way symmetrical approach.

Marketing, of course, is one-sided in the opposite direction: it deliberately molds offerings to meet demand. Because it adapts itself in this way, it does not offer an appropriate model for fundraising. That is, you do not want your donors to determine what it is that you do. Though marketing is, of course, appropriate in the context of the business world where products are concerned, and even in the library world where services are concerned, it is misleading and inappropriate in the context of fundraising.

Because asking someone for money is the scariest part of fundraising for most people, this chapter provides a concrete methodology for conducting the later stages of the cultivation and solicitation process, even though doing so may make development seem more mechanical than it truly is.

Communication is anything but mechanical. In fact, some researchers would argue that little of the meaning of a conversation involves the actual words that are spoken, but rather the spirit in which remarks are offered. According to Deborah Tannen, who researches conversational style and particularly gender differences in communication, men and women generally have different conversational styles and different goals in communication. Women often seek to build rapport, intimacy, and interconnection and avoid the appearance of superiority. Men, on the other hand, seek to protect their independence, are conscious of hierarchy and status, and are inclined to resist what is asked of them. The extent to which you understand the subtleties of different communication styles can have important implications for your success in development, and will justify, for anyone serious about development, the time spent reading about and thinking about them.[2]

THE DONOR'S DECISION-MAKING PROCESS

Decision making is a process. Sometimes it is simple; other times it may be quite elaborate and not immediately comprehensible. But the process can be understood to some extent. And the more we understand it, the more we are able to assist it through our communication with a prospect.

When people make decisions, they go through three phases of thought: the *understanding phase,* the *alternatives phase,* and the *decision phase.*[3] In a fundraising situation, these phases might consist of the following: in the understanding phase, the prospect and the fundraiser interact in order to clarify a gift opportunity. The prospect absorbs information about the gift opportunity, the case for it, its urgency, and the way he might help. If he achieves a clear understanding of the situation, and if he is still interested in it, he will enter the alternatives phase, during which he will sift through his feelings about giving to other causes or not giving at all. Questions such as "what if" and "how about" may arise. He will consciously or unconsciously factor in his *basic issues,* those highly personal, deep-down feelings which everyone brings to every situation and about which we will have more to say presently. A prospect's consideration of his basic issues is a natural part of the process, and you should expect to work with him as the process runs its course. Your careful and patient attention to a person's basic issues are key to getting to a win-win decision for both parties.

The final phase is the decision phase. If the understanding and alternatives phases have been given due care, it should become clear to you and to the prospect whether a gift to your institution is a good fit for each of you. If the fit is right, the decision to give will follow naturally. If the fit is not right, a decision not to give may follow, and that is fine, too.

THE DEVELOPMENT CALL

That stage in your relationship with a donor that might be described as mature contact will be characterized by meetings or "calls" that will lead to solicitation. Make the most of these crucial calls by communicating in the most effective way possible. The communication that goes on in such meetings can be thought of as being of three kinds: *getting information, giving information,* and *getting commitment.*

The first kind of communication, *getting information,* entails asking, learning, and exploring. It involves understanding what you need to know about your prospect's current situation so that you can effectively tell your story. In other words, you want to find out why the prospect might be interested in giving to you. Through careful questioning, you can check on the validity of your assumptions about a person; elicit new information, uncover values, attitudes, and needs that are relevant to the potential gift; and locate the prospect's position in relation to the giving process. Your goal is to have the prospect do most of the talking. One of the great advantages of this approach is that it allows you to identify early on those prospects you should pursue and those you should not pursue. It also allows you to discover prospects' *mind-sets:* their preconceived ideas about your library, your institution, and possibly your cause, based on their past experiences. A person's mind-set is highly subjective, unique to each individual, and is closely linked to personal values and attitudes. No matter how long you have known a person or how many times you have called on her, you should treat every call as if it were your first, since a person's mind-set can change from one meeting to the next in response to circumstances about which you have no knowledge and over which you have no control.[4]

Getting Information: Questioning Techniques

There are various techniques for getting information about your prospect that will help you make the most of each meeting. Following Miller and Heiman, we have identified four types of questions:

1. *Confirmation questions* validate your data and impressions about the prospect or indicate inaccuracies in them.
2. *New information questions* enable you to listen to and absorb the reality of current data; responses to such questions give you information about the prospect's expectations.
3. *Attitude questions* identify the prospect's personal needs, values, and attitudes, and the urgency she feels about taking action on them.
4. *Commitment questions* help you locate your prospect's current position in the gift process—whether she is nearly ready for solicitation or needs more cultivation.

Confirmation questions allow you to test assumptions by asking questions like, "Are you still ... ?" or "Do you continue to ... ?" or "Do you currently remain interested in our plans to do ... ?" Confirmation questions allow you to test the waters to make sure that the prospect's mind-set has not changed.

New information questions allow you to fill in gaps or update information on your prospect. They usually follow the journalistic five *w*'s and an *h*; they are usually questions, that is, that begin with who, what, where, when, why, or how. Be cautious in your use of why, however. Substitute "how" for "why" when you can to avoid the impression that you are questioning the validity of a prospect's statement or the soundness of his judgment. For example, when a potential donor informs you that he collects paperweights, asking him *why* he does so may give him the impression that you think his hobby is peculiar. Asking him *how* he became interested in paperweights is a safer course. It does not run the risk of putting him on the defensive or causing him to clam up.

You can also use new information questions to find out who may have an influence on a prospect's decision to make a gift. We call such people a *giving influence.*[5] Spouses, to use an obvious example, frequently affect a donor's decision. Within foundations and corporations, other people in or connected to the organization have an influence. Whatever the relationship, it is important to involve the *giving influences* in the cultivation and even in the solicitation process if you can.

Attitude questions are perhaps the most important of all because they help you discover how your prospect is feeling personally about your cause. Using attitude questions you can discover what your prospect thinks her association with your cause can do for her. Most people like to talk about their attitudes; they welcome an opportunity to express their feelings. In asking attitude questions, however, you will not want to convey the impression that you are trying to "psych out" the person—to probe her innermost being—or to "get her to like you." It is easy to manage this aspect of the questioning process in a straightforward way by asking what and how questions in conjunction with phrasing that solicits a judgment. "What is your opinion about ... ?" "How did you feel about ... ?" "What was your reaction to ... ?"

The purpose of a commitment question is to learn where in the solicitation process the prospect is and to make it possible for you to move to the next level in the process if appropriate. Commitment questions help you move toward closure. They use key words that relate to future efforts. Verbs like "determine," "plan," and "intend" allow you to focus on what still needs to be done. "Would you be willing to review a proposal outlining x ... ?" "Do I understand that you are interested in making a gift to support the new library if we can present you with some appropriate naming opportunities?"

Obviously, effective communication with your prospect involves much more than running through the four types of questions. You want to maximize the two-way flow of information, allowing for pauses and silence to enhance both your and your prospect's comprehension of the information that is passing between you. To accomplish this, practice strategic silences at various points in the discussion; that is, get into the habit of pausing for three to four seconds after asking a question, and doing the same before responding to an answer. These silences allow your prospect to feel less pressured, to respond at more length, to provide unsolicited information, to explore alternatives (which are so important to the decision-making process), and to focus on the prospect's real wants and needs. They also allow you to formulate further questions, to make your questions more pertinent to the prospect, and to check on body language and other important nonverbal cues.

It is a commonplace of development that after asking for a gift, the requester should never say a word before the prospect has spoken. The idea is that you do not want to let the prospect off the hook by saying something apologetic or lame in order to lower the tension. As with many development ideas, this one also derives from outdated sales approaches and assumes that you are in a sense ambushing your prospect. If you *are* in a situation where you are popping the question, then a silence is probably a good idea. Ideally, however, you have built incremental commitment with your prospect along the way so that it will not be necessary for you to "pop the question"; everyone will know what is going on and where things stand.

Giving Information

One of your goals in a development call is to impart information in a way that will help the prospect understand how to make a reasonable decision about giving to you (or, perhaps, not giving to you). Assume that, on the basis of the information you have already received, you can differentiate your cause from others that may also have a claim on a prospect's attention. You should be ready to discuss your unique strengths in terms of programs, people, collections, technology, or whatever your special niche is. You should also be mentally prepared for the question, "So what?" in relation to your unique strengths since the most impressive list of strengths in the world means nothing if it bears no relation to a prospect's mind-set. Finally, you should be mentally prepared to "prove it!"—that is, to back up your claims.

Getting Commitment

The ultimate goal of any development call is to get a commitment. By "commitment" we do not necessarily mean getting the gift. Often, commitment is incremental until you get the gift. For example, one of your early calls might end with the prospect agreeing to consider a preliminary proposal. The next meeting or meetings might involve discussions of the proposal, and so on, until you eventually get a commitment for a gift. It is important to try to have each meeting conclude with a commitment of some kind so as to avoid "solicitation drift." In this all-too-common scenario, solicitations drag on and on and become a source of frustration and annoyance for all concerned. During each meeting, you should try to come to some kind of mutual understanding. You must also work to resolve any uncertainties, going beyond simply overcoming objections to ensure that both sides—you and the prospect—can feel they have "won."

Certainly, it is not necessary to think of the three types of communication —getting information, giving information, and getting commitment—as being a prescribed sequence you must follow in a conversation; rather, you should move naturally between the different modes in response to the course of the discussion. In some cases, you might even detect that the person you are calling on wants you to cut to the chase. In response, you might move immediately to a commitment question. You should be prepared to be cursory about, or forgo altogether, your spiel—the giving information part of the meeting.

When You Can't Get Commitment

Sometimes you cannot get a commitment. The prospect will not agree to do anything more than "think about it and get back to you." When this happens, it is often because the prospect does not consider his support of your cause as offering a winning situation for him. Here you come up against prospects' deepest values and attitudes, or their *basic issues*. These might have to do with their perceived status of your cause, their attitudes about the recognition they will receive, or their fears of losing control of a situation. These feelings may be so personal that they may never come out in the open. You will know that you are in trouble, however, when you encounter some or all of the following symptoms, listed in order of their severity:

Hesitation ——> Questioning Attitude ——> Grunt and Groan ——>
Argument ——> Hostility or Passive Resistance

Generally, once a person has reached the grunt-and-groan stage, it is very difficult to turn things around. But assuming things have not gotten to an irreversible point, it is sometimes possible to put things back on track by asking questions that uncover basic issues. "Are there any concerns that need to be resolved?" "Is there anything about which you are uncertain (puzzled, uncomfortable, unclear)?" Sometimes, however, it is not possible to uncover a person's basic issues. In these cases it is often useful to seek insight from a reliable third party.

Credibility

In Chapter 1 we noted that, by virtue of their position and the prestige that accrues to it, library directors have a great deal of credibility. This credibility is, in a sense, inherited capital: you have not had to do anything to acquire it other than to land your job. And this credibility will help you with donors.

Yet in most cases, more will be required. Though people will be impressed by you in your role as the leader of your library and a high-level representative of your institution, you will usually have to establish an additional degree of trust before they will make a commitment to you. You will have to earn this additional credibility when you go into a meeting with your prospect.

Here are some guidelines for earning credibility: (1) be yourself; (2) do not come across as a know-it-all, give pat answers, or appear to be arrogant or self-aggrandizing; (3) be precise in your questions; and (4) listen attentively to answers.[6] Regarding this last point, do not be too quick or too literal in interpreting a prospect's answers to your questions; listen for nuances. Try to listen to not just what is said, but what is meant.

Getting the Appointment

The approach to getting an appointment varies depending on your relationship with each donor and how far along they are in the cultivation process. Remember that each prospect is unique. That said, there are three types of situations you will commonly face in making an appointment with a prospect. Listed in order of increasing difficulty, they are: (1) when your relationship with the donor is mature; (2) when it is completely new; and (3) when it is somewhere in between.

When you know someone well, and you know that it is time to solicit him (and he probably knows it, too), use an open approach. Be honest and forthright whenever possible without showing your entire hand: "I would like to come to see you to discuss your support of the library." The prospect may try to pin you down at this point, saying something like, "You are going to ask me for money, aren't you?" Try not to tell all or you will have no reason for the appointment. Instead say, "I do want to talk specifically about your support for the library, but what we have to talk about is far too important for a phone call. When might we get together?" Another technique is to have an assistant or development officer call to make the appointment for you.

A different scenario arises when you do not know someone well or at all. You do not want to scare the person off by bringing up fundraising long before you actually want to ask for a gift. At this point, you are merely exploring possibilities and building a relationship. Though you certainly cannot say, "I would like to see you in order to explore building a relationship with you," you can say, "I am the new director and I would really like to meet you because . . ." or "I would like to seek your advice about . . ." or "I am going to be in your area, and I would very much like to update you on what we are doing in the library." Another time-honored technique for getting in the door of someone you do not know is to have someone who knows the person open the door for you by calling him and asking him to see you.

The issue of getting an appointment is most difficult in those relationships that are neither entirely new nor old. In these cases, how open should you be in stating your purpose in seeking an appointment? Unfortunately, there is no clear-cut way to resolve this problem. You do not want to use an oblique excuse to see someone and then spring a different agenda on her once you are in her office. You may have to use a nonthreatening reason to get the meeting, but, if so, you will not want to give the prospect the sense, by completely ignoring the ostensible purpose of the meeting, that she has been set up. Good questioning is essential in this type of call. When it is appropriate to give information, you will probably want to describe in general terms whatever opportunity it is that you want help with. If the response is favorable, and other feedback is positive, too, you might decide to ask the person, "Would you be interested in considering a proposal to do X?"

Asking for the Gift

The most crucial call of all is the one in which you may ask for a gift. Perhaps it is helpful to know that many successful fundraisers rehearse their solicitations. If you feel comfortable doing so, consider role-playing with your development director. It might be beneficial to think through the four types of questions and come up with one or more confirmation, new information, attitude, and commitment questions. You might also want to remind yourself to be alert to the elements of the decision-making process, especially the understanding phase and the questioning-of-alternatives phase. Remind yourself to highlight your unique strengths and to employ silences.

If your fundraiser is going along on the call, decide in advance who is going to say what. There are two very good reasons for having the fundraiser or a second person along on solicitation calls. One is that the other person can artfully fill in any gaps in your presentation. The second is that she can assist you if things get off track or if your nerve fails you. In the latter case, for example, she might say, "The director has told you that we need X. Now we would like to talk to you about making this happen."

If there is a suitable volunteer, one who is a peer of your prospect and has some fundraising experience, consider involving him in the call instead of your development officer. A volunteer fundraiser who has already made a financial commitment to the library and who is a friend or respected colleague of a prospect can be a powerful influence. In particular, prospects who are first-time givers often respond to the model of another's actions. Just be careful not to depend too much on having the right peer: established donors who are willing to participate in solicitations are much less plentiful than many people involved in fundraising would have you believe.[7]

What do you say when you ask someone for money? The word "consider" is often very useful in these situations, as in: "Would you consider making a gift of $100,000?"; or: "As you know, we are trying to raise $4 million, and we are hoping you might consider giving $500,000."

Always mention a specific amount; do not leave your prospect to guess it. Your research on a prospect is supposed to give you a sense of the appropriate amount for which to ask, but it does not always. In these cases, you have little choice but to make your best guess. One approach is to first ask high and then discuss lower amounts if necessary. Many fundraisers believe that prospects are flattered to be asked for too much. Though this is sometimes true, extravagant requests are not flattering, so do not go overboard when you decide on a figure.

How do you know when to ask? Timing is critical. All the preparation in the world will mean nothing if your prospect's financial situation has suddenly undergone a reversal. For this reason, it is often a good idea to begin a meeting with a confirmation question relating to timing. However, "Is this still a good time to talk?" might be a bit obsequious. Listen carefully to opening chit-chat about "how things are going." Often you will discover hints about whether the timing is good or bad, and you may get the opportunity to talk about problems the prospect may be having.

If you conduct the later stages of the cultivation and solicitation process as we suggest, you should know exactly where you stand and when to ask. But what if things have not gone as we suggest, for whatever reason? Use your instinct. If it does not feel right, listen to this feeling. You may be sensing that the person needs more cultivation. But beware of mistaking this feeling for your own fear of asking; many cultivations go on far too long for just this reason.

Another point about timing: ideally, over the course of the cultivation of a prospect, you have developed a *reciprocal context,* a term used by persuasion expert Robert Cialdini to describe a relationship that has become mutually beneficial to both parties.[8] In such a context, the prospect is aware of the direct or indirect benefits he derives from your institution, and he is assured that benefits will continue to flow in return for his support. For example, say you have invited a prospect to be your guest at several very special events. The prospect, for his part, has introduced someone potentially important to you and has also hosted an event in his home. In other words, you have been exchanging benefits. A proper reciprocal context should develop naturally over the course of the cultivation of your relationship. Be careful not to ask for a gift before the proper context has been established.

There is another psychological context important to a successful solicitation that Cialdini calls *friendship/liking.*[9] Common sense tells us that people prefer to comply with the requests of people they know and like. There is an important caveat to this principle, however: never pretend to be building a friendship with someone and then violate the rules by which true friends interact. This is manipulation, and it will be recognized for what it is.

It is a good idea after every call to evaluate how the meeting went. You will gain confidence as you see yourself becoming a more skillful fund-raiser. After each meeting, it is also very important to note what information was exchanged and what commitments were made on each side. If your development director was present, he will prepare a written record of the meeting (a call report) for the files. He will also draft for you, if appropriate, a follow-up letter to the prospect thanking him for his time and summarizing the meeting. If the development director was not present, he can debrief you and then prepare the call report and follow-up letter.

The fundraising methodology described in this chapter is an honorable one. *You* are not scoring; *everyone* is winning. This approach allows you not only to keep your dignity, but to have a bit of fun. And the added bonus is that it results in gifts to your library.

NOTES

1. This approach is epitomized by Joe Girard's *How to Sell Anything to Anybody* (New York: Warner Books, 1977).

2. See, for example, Deborah Tannen, *You Just Don't Understand: Women and Men in Conversation* (New York: William Morrow and Company, 1990).

3. These terms and the others introduced in this chapter, unless otherwise noted, are taken from Robert B. Miller and Stephen E. Heiman, *Conceptual Selling* (New York: Warner Books, 1987). Their work provides a useful explanation of current approaches to sales. Many aspects of their approach are relevant to development; much of this chapter draws on their ideas and terminology and adapts it to fundraising.

4. Cf. Miller and Heiman, pp. 41–42.

5. Ibid., p. 71.

6. Ibid., pp. 227–230.

7. See Kathleen S. Kelly, *Fund Raising and Public Relations: A Critical Analysis* (Hillsdale, N.J.: Lawrence Erlbaum, 1991), on the "myth of the volunteer solicitor," pp. 143–149.

8. Robert B. Cialdini, "What Leads to Yes: Applying the Psychology of Influence to Fund Raising, Alumni Relations, and PR," *CASE Currents* (January 1987): 49.

9. Ibid., p. 51.

CHAPTER **6** Fundraising with
Friends Groups

The Role of Friends in Development

At various points we have stressed the importance of understanding your library's purposes and uniqueness as you design its development program, and we have explored ways to design fundraising programs to fit a particular niche and to suit a library director's individual talents and abilities. When you consider the role of your library Friends group, being aware of the uniqueness of your development program is no less important.

Different Friends groups require different strategies. Your challenge as a library director is to understand the strategy that is most appropriate to your situation. For example, some Friends groups are separate nonprofit entities; legally and practically, they are independent and not answerable to the library director. Many such groups, while they may be only minimally interested in fundraising, are, however, effective lobbyists and activists or provide other valuable services to the library that should be fostered and encouraged. If you have such a group, it might be best to look elsewhere for volunteer help with fundraising. In other situations, however, Friends groups are under the direct control of the library, so their members can be recruited and oriented to serve a development purpose. This chapter concerns the latter scenario: how to raise money with your Friends group if that is appropriate and if it is possible given your unique situation.

If you want to use your Friends organization to raise money, manage it as a development-oriented group. Managed in this way, it can generate moderate income, occasionally provide a source of major-donor prospects and a mechanism for their cultivation, and be fun for members and library staff. When a development program does not include a major-gifts component, the Friends will essentially be the heart of your development effort. If you have opted for a full-scale development program, the Friends can provide a mechanism for cultivating and stewarding major-gift prospects and donors. Earlier, we used the analogy of the fundraising swimming pool to describe how the Friends can perform this function.

Though Friends groups are often thought to be essential to library development, we hold more skeptical views on this subject. We can envision an ambitious, effective major-gifts library fundraising program without any Friends group because a Friends group is not central to a major-gifts program. There are at least two reasons for this. First, conventional wisdom notwithstanding, Friends groups are not the only entry point into an organization for major-gift prospects; most of your major donors will not come to you through the Friends. Second, while it is true that the Friends serve public relations and advocacy functions and sometimes provide volunteer workers for libraries, these benefits, plus a minimal financial return, make a Friends group a dubious endeavor from a development perspective. Generally speaking, only Friends groups that serve a development purpose can accrue fundraising benefits to libraries that outweigh the considerable effort they require from the staff.

Library Friends groups tend to be either of two kinds: traditional Friends groups that serve as a club to generate goodwill for the library and those that, in addition to serving a goodwill function, form an integral part of a fundraising program. For purposes of comparison, the following list identifies traits of each of these two types of Friends groups.

Club-Oriented Friends	Development-Oriented Friends
Form a club	Serve a development purpose
Buy books for the library	Raise endowment
Are left to run themselves	Are run by the library
Are assigned, if at all, to librarians with other responsibilities	Are assigned to development staff
Hold events that focus on operations or esoteric topics	Host fun activities
Build membership the populist way: bigger = better	Recruit MAGIC members
See the library director playing a minor role	See the library director as the focal point
Comprise the only annual-giving activity	Form part of the annual-giving base

Whether your Friends group is the heart of your development program or only an element of it, the organization can be designed and managed to accomplish development goals, particularly if it is under the direct control of the library. How is this done? Since a Friends group takes its character from the unique people in and around the library, different groups can succeed in different ways. But if a Friends group is to make a truly positive contribution to your development program it should incorporate some basic principles that we believe hold true in nearly every setting.

THE FRIENDS AND THE DEVELOPMENT PURPOSE

The main purpose of the Friends group should be to support the library financially. Development goals must be kept constantly before the group, both at the board level and the member level. Updates on fundraising goals should always be agenda items at board meetings. Activities, such as fund-raising events, should be linked to dollar goals. Events should pay for themselves in most cases. Membership fees should be on the higher, rather than the lower, side. Prospective board members should be clear about the expectations of them for meeting attendance, duties, and financial com-mitment anticipated by the board and the library director. People asked to be on the board should receive a letter from the director containing a statement that specifically addresses these commitments (though some flexibility is allowed here). For example:

> As a Board member, you will be asked to attend quarterly meetings and other events as often as you can. The Board and I will also ask for your help and advice in fundraising and public relations matters, as well as ask that you maintain your own financial commitment to the Library.

The Friends group should not function merely as a bibliophilic club whose activities are largely social and whose main occupation is organiz-ing periodic gatherings and outings. In this all-too-common scenario, the library ends up supporting the support group. In forming your board, avoid "clubbies"; rather, fill it with highly visible, hands-off people who want to support the broad goals of the library's development program.

The Friends and Endowment

In order to keep fundraising as the primary purpose of the Friends and to give the group an ambitious goal to strive for, the group should have specific fundraising goals that reflect the priorities of the library. There are a number of options toward which a Friends group can direct its fundrais-ing efforts, but we would recommend two areas of focus in most situations. First, a Friends group should certainly raise enough money from its mem-bership fees to keep itself running; second, surplus funds should be placed into an ever-growing endowment fund for the library.

Raising money for endowment provides many advantages over other traditional uses of Friends' funds: (1) the group is likely to be more satisfied in the long run if it is engaged in raising endowment, both through its collective gift and through individual contributions; (2) Friends can experience the growth of an endowment, whereas merely adding books now and then to shelves, for example, tends to have an episodic and unsustained quality; (3) since the fund stays open it is always present to provide a focus for the group; (4) it can be named for the Friends, thereby providing recognition; (5) it provides a legacy for a group that will answer the question, "What did those people ever do besides have meetings and throw parties?"; and (6) periodic challenge grants can provide further incentive for giving. Giving to endowment allows the return on the endowment to be integrated into the long-range collection development plan of the library, leaving acquisition decisions where they should be left—in the hands of the librarians.

Currently, many Friends groups direct their monies to purposes other than endowment, but most of these have drawbacks. For example, some groups spend their funds on book purchases. The practice of allowing the Friends to shop for books or to add specific volumes to the collection on a regular basis sends the wrong message. It suggests that the Friends group can be involved in operational decision making, namely, the acquisition of books for the library, and this is an involvement you want to avoid. Some of the Friends will be bored by ambitions as limited as these, especially those Friends who are not bibliophiles. Another way Friends groups direct their funds is toward small capital projects, such as an exhibit case or a preservation project. These often have the undesirable effect of setting too narrowly the Friends' sights. On the other hand, more ambitious capital projects such as buildings are usually beyond the reach of Friends groups.

Raising funds for endowment has the advantage of being both general in its aim (funds can be spent on a wide range of things) and specific in its focus (building the principal of the library's endowment). Endowment gives the library needed long-term resources that can be utilized by the library staff in the most advantageous way while leaving a legacy of the Friends' support.

Managing the Friends

If you want your Friends group both to serve a development purpose and to complement the goals of the library, the impetus for its management should come from the library staff. Ideas for new board members, events, and appropriate fundraising goals should come primarily from the library director and the development officer in charge of the Friends. (If you have anyone else in your library who is interested, use their input, too.) The day-to-day work of the Friends should be done primarily by development staff members in the library. If your Friends' board has ideas, you should certainly listen to them, but you should not allow the board to create its own agenda. Rather, you should develop a format into which their ideas may be inserted and in which their contacts may be used. For example, you might sponsor a program of quarterly literary luncheons; in such a case, a board member who can supply, through personal acquaintance, a famous author as a speaker for a luncheon would be encouraged to do so, but the series should not depend on such contacts. And though the president of the Friends' board convenes its meetings and receives due deference from the director, the development staff put together the agenda.

Treat board members as counselors, and manage board meetings much as you would an advisory council meeting by giving updates on important library issues. The key agenda item at board meetings should always concern development. The board should focus on such matters as recruitment of new members (hosting intimate dinner parties at their homes to bring in new people, for example), discussions of recent major gifts, and, in a university setting, efforts to tie in the group's activities to parents' funds and telemarketing programs. Your board members and other volunteers should provide money, bring new members into the organization, and use their contacts to benefit the library. If they want to tinker with the Friends organization itself or the library—for example, if they want to revise the Friends' bylaws or review library policy—you probably have the wrong volunteers.

Friends' Activities

Friends should host events that have a relatively broad appeal and should package these events in an attractive manner. For example, activities in this category might include openings of library exhibits, annual galas, and luncheons with noted authors. Realize, however, that the name recognition of your featured guest (or guests) makes a huge difference in drawing people to events. If you live in a major city, you can tie into authors' promotional tours through their publishers or agents.

Events of a more intellectual or academic nature should be sponsored outside the sphere of the Friends. Esoteric, scholarly talks do not fit the definition of fun for most people, nor do visits to binderies or narrowly specialized collections, nor do, most certainly, events focusing on library operations. This is not to disparage such activities but, in planning events, you should aim to appeal to as broad an audience as you can. You are likely to be more successful in attracting donors if you can present your Friends group as being a lively, culturally sophisticated organization.

Recruiting Members with MAGIC

If your Friends group is to support your library financially, its membership should include those who not only have the inclination to help but the means to do so. Remember to consider the MAGIC formula (means, age, givers, involvement, contacts) when thinking about building the Friends. Friends groups are a great deal of work; bigger is not necessarily better! You should welcome Friends at all financial levels, but it is not useful to have a membership that consists only of small givers. Expanding the number of higher level donors, as opposed to boosting the numbers of support group members, is your true goal.

The Library Director as the Focal Point

As with all aspects of a development program, an effective Friends group depends on leadership from the library director. While the leadership of the Friends' president is important, the president should be positioned to support the library director, who is the CEO of the library. Only the library director can provide the group with the consistent, long-term, big-picture leadership necessary to guide it on a course that fully complements the overall development plan of the library. Just as the director should avoid getting overly entangled in the quotidian details of the library, so in working with the Friends board should he focus (and keep the board focused) on the big picture. The library director should never get involved in the details of event management, such as caterers and florists. In board meetings, he should not be overly concerned about bylaws; he may use them when it is useful for him to do so and may ignore them the rest of the time. It is equally unnecessary to provide the board with detailed reports of income and expenditures. This policy will likely agree with the board members, who will appreciate being kept informed of basic library goals and concerns, but who might well be bored by such minutiae.

The Friends as Part of a Broader Donor Base

In a university setting, the development person in charge of the Friends should work with the central development office to coordinate the library's fundraising goals with those of other annual-giving groups or activities. In some situations, there may be opportunities for tie-ins with the parents' association, regional giving clubs, and the telemarketing effort. These tie-ins take a great deal of effort and often require political clout; they are not easy to establish, since other fundraisers in a university may also have their eye on these potential funding sources.

Another activity that can broaden the library's annual-giving base is an end-of-year direct-mail solicitation, which might be targeted to the Friends, all donors of gifts-in-kind, and any other list of prospects you can put together. Other, similar programs might include a memorial and commemorative gifts program (in which people make donations that result in bookplates being placed in new acquisitions to honor someone) or named endowment programs (in which people make donations in an area of special interest). Some libraries have had success forging fundraising partnerships with the athletic program. Indiana University, for example, benefited from the support of the popular basketball coach Bobby Knight, who issued appeals on behalf of the library.

In a public-library setting, similar kinds of base-broadening strategies can be devised. For example, it may be possible to purchase or exchange mailing lists with cultural organizations in your area. Other potentially fertile sources of annual-gift donors include library user lists, especially if they can be screened electronically (see Chapter 3), lists of book-sale and gift-shop customers, vendor lists, and membership lists of book-collecting groups.

If the Friends group is the heart of your fundraising program, and if it is well managed, it can fit nicely with our definition of library development as *a carefully orchestrated, purposive effort to raise substantial sums of money by identifying and cultivating potential donors and by soliciting gifts from them when their goals and wishes are congruent with the library's goals and priorities*. A proper understanding of the purpose of a Friends group and the proper use of your fundraiser, who acts as a Sherpa guide, can allow you to obtain maximum results with minimal effort on your part. If, on the other hand, your Friends group is an ancillary part of a program directed primarily to facilitating a major-gifts effort, the organization can provide a ready-made body to which you can attach both prospects you are cultivating for a major gift and donors who have already made a gift. As we explained in chapters 2 and 3 using the swimming pool analogy, the Friends can offer a milieu for allowing different people to come together, to mix, and to share and encourage each other's interest in the library.

QUESTIONS OFTEN ASKED ABOUT FRIENDS GROUPS

How do I decide what benefits to offer members?

In developing benefits for your Friends, try to package your group in a way that will be interesting to a wide audience. Events that have a broad appeal bring new people in contact with the library and help to counteract the "clubbiness" that specialized, narrowly focused events encourage. The right names and labels are extremely important in making your events appealing. They tell your audience in the briefest possible way what the activity is about, and they carry with them the image that you want to project. Rather than merely arranging events in an ad hoc way, try to create a series with a catchy name that appeals to their interests.

The list of traditional Friends benefits—a library card, bookplates in library books, a newsletter, invitations to events—may work fine for your low-end members. For high-level benefits (usually $5,000 or more), be creative and generous. In a university setting, try to tie into other groups on campus that offer access and benefits of their own. The University Associates group often offers broad-range perquisites that appeal to high-level donors.

What membership levels should I offer?

Provide a full range of giving opportunities for potential donors to your library, but do not start your Friends memberships too low. Some Friends groups charge $25 for their basic membership; it costs most institutions more than that in overhead just to process the check.

How important are membership benefits?

This issue has two sides. On the one hand, remember that your members are givers. They are giving to your library, not just buying a product, and you want to encourage them to think in those terms. Most will not care so much about their benefits as about whether their gift is going to a good end.

On the other hand, benefits can be very important in reinforcing your case for support. People who care about benefits really seem to care a great deal about them. In fact, you will find that your low-end members are the ones who care most about their benefits. Major donors will, as a whole, not be the ones to call when the newsletter is late or when they have failed to receive their membership lapel pin.

Array your benefits by membership level in a way that will encourage members to upgrade their membership to as high a level as possible, but that will still allow them to feel that they are getting their money's worth. There is always a fine line between offering people benefits commensurate with their membership and getting bogged down in too many benefits and activities. Try to keep your benefits list lean.

How should I handle the billing of membership dues?

Many groups bill their Friends members on an annual basis, timing the renewal to coincide with the month a member originally joined. We believe this approach has drawbacks; we prefer concentrating membership renewal notices to begin during the same month each year. Annual billing saves staff time, makes the status of the membership renewal easier to monitor, and frees up the remainder of the year for other appeals to the membership. Unless they join in the month of your first renewal notice, this billing cycle sometimes results in people getting more than a year's worth of membership (never less), which is nice for them and easy for you.

What about Friends publications?

Many Friends groups publish a newsletter and some publish a journal as well; to most people who support libraries, such publications are attractive and appropriate benefits. If you offer a newsletter and/or a journal, they should serve a development purpose. This emphasis need not result in a heavy-handed approach, with an overemphasis on fundraising goals or appeals for support. But it does mean that the primary "people news" should center on your volunteers, not your staff. Another appropriate focus is on interesting news and projects, not on services or scholarly matters. Instead, the publications should feature news items, projects, and donors that are key to your development program. This will happen naturally if they are produced by your development staff, rather than by the Friends themselves or by your librarians. Unfortunately, newsletters and other publications are a great deal of work and can take away from the more directly productive development activities of the library staff. If you are going to take on a newsletter, make sure you have adequate staffing; and if you are considering more involved publications, it is doubly important to be sure that you have the people, time, and money necessary for the task.

How much income can a Friends group be expected to generate?

While acknowledging that the uniqueness principle is always operating, and that different Friends groups in different libraries will raise different amounts of money, an active Friends group can be expected to generate about $25,000 per year in membership dues. Many groups make much more, especially those that are the sole source of library cards for the public. Once expenses are deducted from income, however, you can see that dues alone generally do not make a Friends group cost-effective. This is why the Friends should, ideally, serve a broader development purpose in relation to a major-gifts effort and should endeavor to bring additional support to the library, especially through efforts to interest other giving groups in the library.

If the library card is the major attraction for joining a Friends group, how can the Friends also serve a development purpose?

Library-card fees can provide a good base of income for a Friends group, thus allowing for flexibility in planning development events, producing development publications, mounting direct-mail marketing campaigns, and the like. These activities, in turn, can enable the group to contribute more support to the library than might otherwise be the case.

People who join the Friends primarily to get a library card, however, may not be particularly interested in supporting the library. The result may be that you end up with two separate interest groups within your Friends: "true Friends" and "library-card Friends." Though it can be very difficult to distinguish between the two, especially if you have a large mailing list, it is the "true Friends" on whom you should focus your development attentions. Those members will provide the leadership of your development-oriented Friends group. Avoid, if you possibly can, creating "library-card Friends."

Should students be encouraged to join the Friends and/or participate in their activities?

In academic libraries these questions often arise: "Should we recruit students to join the Friends?" and "Why don't more students come to our events?" In regard to the first question, ask yourself, as you should regarding every other prospect or prospect population, "Do they have MAGIC?" Clearly, in the case of students, the answer is usually no. Of course this does not mean that a student's membership would not be welcome, but only that the student population is not a productive focus for Friends' membership efforts.

In regard to the second question, keep in mind the purpose of your Friends group: fundraising. Then remember that most students have academic priorities of their own that may or may not align with the activities of your Friends. That is their right. What we think students "should" do with their time is, ultimately, irrelevant.

How important is a Friends board?

If you have attended any development workshops or done any reading in development, you have undoubtedly been advised about the importance of having "good boards." Those giving this advice usually have in mind not support-group boards such as the board of a library Friends organization, but rather boards of trustees of nonprofit organizations. As we said in Chapter 1, the library setting is considerably different in that the library director is far more important than board members in a successful fundraising program.

Be that as it may, your Friends board is important for a couple of reasons. First, its leadership is obviously important to the vitality of your Friends group. You will want to recruit the best people you can to your board, especially ones with MAGIC, and you will want to devote the bulk of your time to the *board* of your Friends, not the membership at large. Second, your Friends board is a formal, exclusive group that, if managed correctly, can provide its members with a good deal of status, something most people seek and relish. In this way, the board is an excellent vehicle for cultivating donor prospects. At the same time, realize that your very best donors and prospects will be, and should be, at a level beyond the Friends board; in a university setting, for example, they will be trustee-level individuals.

What about support groups for branch libraries or units?

As specialized units and branches in our libraries become more and more desperate for funds, the people running them begin to think of fundraising. Having little or no experience with raising major gifts, most librarians believe that fundraising means having a Friends group. As we have noted, however, this is a misconception—the drawbacks from a development standpoint to Friends groups being numerous.

If you are contemplating the formation of a support group for a specialized library or branch, work through the following exercise first, and remember that Friends groups produce mostly low-level gifts.

1. Examine the leadership of the branch or specialized library. Galvanizing a Friends group requires that the head of the library it supports have charismatic personal qualities and unequivocal commitment. It requires an exciting vision and an opportunity. Do these things exist or is there simply a perceived need for more money, more activity, and more visibility?

2. Estimate the costs of running a Friends group. A Friends group usually entails activities, newsletters, and other benefits. It requires a board and communication with that board. If you analyze your staff costs and expenditures in even a rough way, you will quickly determine that most Friends groups end up *costing* you money.

3. Make a list of your most viable potential Friends members, divide the total number in half (since less than half of them will actually join your group), and multiply the number by $50 (an estimate of your average gift). The total probably will not add up to much or even begin to approach the dollar level you are looking for to solve your financial crisis. Chances are the amount you need is well out of range of even the most robust annual-giving group.

4. Are the names on your list from item 3 the same names that are on the roster of the larger Friends group of your main or central library? If so, these people probably already think they are helping your specialized library in some indirect way. They certainly do not need another Friends group for their cultivation as donors. Also, ask whether the people on your list are the same people who are involved in similar groups in your area. If they are, they may have reached their limit so far as your cause is concerned.

In almost every case, those concerned with raising money for a branch or specialized library would be better off cultivating and soliciting a handful of major-gift prospects rather than forming and managing a Friends group. Think of two or three people who are connected to your specialized library in some way and who are capable of making a large gift. Shape your fundraising plans around these people. Discuss a strategy with someone who understands development and concentrate your time and energies on these prospects.

What if my Friends group is totally focused on special collections?

There are several scenarios in which special collections becomes the focal point of a Friends group. In some cases, a library's Friends group is literally the Friends of Special Collections; they are one and the same, and the group may be so entrenched that it would not be feasible to expand it to encompass the general libraries. If you want a general library Friends group, you are often left with the difficult alternative of establishing a splinter group. Unfortunately, it can be difficult for the two groups to avoid competing for prospects, resources, and staff time. The best advice in this situation is not to start a general Friends group since you do not need one for your development program and since it would be hard to compete with the existing group.

In another scenario, the general library Friends tend to focus on special collections because it is thought that (1) special collections has the most interesting materials to share with Friends members or (2) special collections has been assigned the management of the Friends. Both of these situations reflect outdated thinking. In regard to the first situation, Friends programs should not necessarily be focused on materials in the collections, since such programs may tend to involve narrowly bibliographic concerns and to encourage the sorts of clubby qualities your group should avoid. If your programs always revolve around materials in special collections, you probably need more creativity in developing your Friends programs (see Chapter 7). In regard to the second situation, management of the Friends does not belong with special collections; if the Friends group is to serve a development function, it should be supervised by the library director and the development staff.

In the university setting, another scenario involves groups that have been organized to support off-campus special collections. These special collections may either be administered by the central special collections or be independent branches. In the former instance, you may not wish to take on the burden of running a separate Friends group. In the latter, we see no problem with support groups for branches if your purposes and uniqueness warrant them and if there is adequate development staffing support.

What if the same small group of people attends each Friends event?

It could be that your events are not fun for most people. If you want, or must have, a Friends group, enhance its offerings. Libraries are not in the business of hosting clubs, and it takes almost as much effort and money to host a reception for 25 as it does to host one for 200. You are better off having a few new prospects to lunch every week than you are trying to run a full-fledged Friends group for the same 25 faces.

There is one possible exception: it could be that your Friends group is small and unchanging, but that it has all of the right people in it. That is, the people who are involved are prospects of the highest order. In this case, they should be involved in the task of expanding the membership. They should be identifying other potential prospects and helping you to evaluate and involve them.

What if I don't have a Friends group?

Count your blessings! You can begin one from scratch if you want to, or if you decide you do not need a Friends group (see our previous chapters), you can save yourself the complexities of its management. The trend in development is away from Friends groups.

What if my Friends group seems hopeless from a development perspective?

First you must decide if the group benefits the library sufficiently in nonmonetary ways to make it a worthwhile endeavor. As you know by now, we are skeptical about the value of a group that does not raise funds for the library. However, if you decide that your group is worth continuing for whatever reason, be realistic about your expectations of the group and be prepared to justify its existence on its own terms.

What if, however, you privately feel that you would be better off without your Friends group? If so, you will have a difficult time mustering the energy and commitment to revitalize it. Though there has been a great deal said and written about revitalizing a Friends group, it is actually a very difficult thing to accomplish. If you decide that your group is more trouble than it is worth, you are to be commended for taking the courageous step of dissolving it. Unfortunately, in many cases this solution is not very realistic given how prevalent and well-established most Friends groups are. Though they can limp along for years, they do not die easily.

If you must keep your Friends group and revitalize it, the best thing to do is to put a development professional in charge of it or take direct charge of it yourself. This will send a clear message about your intentions and will give you the opportunity to make the necessary changes to turn the Friends into a productive endeavor that complements your development program.

CHAPTER 7 **Black Holes or Black Ties?**

How to Make Your Events Worth
the Trouble

To astronomers, an *event* is a point in space-time; an *event horizon* is the boundary of a black hole, a region where the gravitational pull is so great that nothing, not even light, can escape from its overpowering force. Everyone who has planned black-tie galas, conferences, or other large-scale events has likely encountered a similar horizon. Special events, especially those that are large, but often small ones, too, assume an inexorable force of their own, creating an atmosphere that sucks in our time and energy, sometimes beyond the point of no return.

Several kinds of library events can be useful development tools, but it is critical to understand how to think about events, how to know when they are in line with your purposes and fit your niche, and when they may become more trouble to the library director and staff than they merit.

In this chapter we look at events from the point of view of the library director, who makes the ultimate decisions about whether an event will effectively contribute to the library's development goals. Rather than focus on the nuts and bolts of event planning (which, in any case, are matters for staff), we describe how the development staff and the library director work together in order to get the most mileage out of events. First, we explain what the library director can expect from the staff with respect to events. Then, we discuss the five things every library director should know to make development events effective. Finally, we dissect an actual library fundraiser, not only in order to illustrate how to orchestrate events but also to point out pitfalls. Throughout the chapter, remember that, as a library director, your role is to keep your eye on the big picture; as with anything else in development, you should be able confidently to delegate to your development officer the nitty-gritty aspects of events.

WHAT TO EXPECT FROM THE DEVELOPMENT STAFF

In addition to managing the details of an event, the development staff should attend to the following:

1. *The staff should brief the director beforehand* and sketch out some specific goals for the event. They might, for instance, ask that you speak to certain people and obtain information from them (usually information involving MAGIC) or communicate specific things to them.
2. *The staff should also review your script with you,* or any formal remarks they have prepared for you.
3. *The staff should schedule a debriefing* after the event to which anyone who worked at the event will be invited. The staff will make note of important things that happened, and will discuss follow-up strategies. Since you are the tone-setter for the library, your evaluation of the event will be useful feedback for the development staff.

THE LIBRARY DIRECTOR'S CONCERNS

As the library director, you need to bear in mind five ideas in order to have your events serve a development purpose:

1. *Understand the relationship of events to development* and have realistic expectations of what events can do for you.
2. *Understand the four types of library development events and their purposes.*
3. *Understand the value of content and feeling in events.*
4. *Understand the role you play in setting tone, style, and image.*
5. *Master the art of effectiveness in group situations.*

Understand the Relationship of Events to Development

Though it is true that fundraising often involves events, it is a mistake to identify or equate events with development, as many libraries and other nonprofit organizations frequently do. (This misconception is also implicit in a good deal of the development literature that discusses events.) The best advice is to have a realistic expectation of what you can and cannot accomplish using events in your development program.

First, be aware that most development events do not raise money at all; they expend it in the hope that the cultivation of those who attend will lead to their giving later on. Even many events that are intended to raise money have little or no financial return after expenses and effort are taken into consideration.

Another drawback with group gatherings is that they generally provide only superficial contact with guests. Most events facilitate only the early stages in the development cycle—identification and initial involvement. The library director, as the head fundraiser, needs to concentrate her energies on the later phases of the development cycle—on mature cultivation and solicitation—which involve one-to-one contacts. Be sure that you do not overemphasize group gatherings as a way of avoiding the more personal, intimate contact involved in mature cultivation.

Still, events can serve useful ends. Events are a good way to introduce new people to your library program and to keep in touch with your supporters and friends. They are a good way to entertain your prospects while educating them about your needs. If they are in line with your purposes and your niche, events can be a useful part of your development effort.

Understand the Four Types of Events

Library development events fall into four categories: Friends events, cultivation events, acknowledgment or recognition events, and fundraisers or benefits.[1] Each type of event has a different purpose and should be designed accordingly; nevertheless, they each should be held in the library if at all possible. Take advantage of and highlight your facilities in planning events. In most cases, the link between an event and your library will not be forged in your guests' minds unless the event is held in the library. An exception to this general principle might be outings that the Friends group arranges.

Friends of the Library Events

The primary purpose of these events is to fulfill your promise to provide activities for people who join your Friends group; events are benefits of membership. But, to be worth the trouble, a Friends event must be more than just a party or lecture and must be used for general cultivation and stewardship activities. Friends events should provide ready-made vehicles for involvement and thus serve a purpose beyond the obligatory one. As was emphasized in the last chapter, these events should be appealing and entertaining rather than perfunctory.

Cultivation Events

The purpose of a cultivation event is to get acquainted with a group of people in hopes of identifying and further involving those who are likely to become donors. For purposes of this discussion, we are making a distinction between a Friends event that can partly be used for cultivation purposes and a cultivation event per se. Examples of the latter might include an event for targeted segments of your community, such as the high-tech community, book collectors, or any other specific group.

Cultivation events expose people to you and your library, but it is difficult at events (cultivation or otherwise) to get to know someone in a way that permits you to initiate the next step. To make any event worthwhile, you must be skilled both at working a room and at initiating follow-up steps afterward. In the majority of cases, you will use your own time and your staff's time more effectively if you employ a more personal approach to get to know someone. Invite them to lunch or dinner, for instance.

Volunteers or faculty members may suggest that the library sponsor a cultivation event for a particular interest group. They will insist that a certain segment of the community has lots of money and that you should "go after it." Many people, when they think of fundraising, automatically think of cultivation events. They assume that initial contacts must occur in large gatherings. Sometimes they are right. But often this view reflects a lack of knowledge about the ways development works. The trick is to be able to recognize when a cultivation event might be beneficial and when it would be a waste of energy and resources.

Recognition Events

The purpose of a recognition event is to publicly thank a donor or donors for a gift by means of a ceremonial expression of gratitude. Frequently these events involve official acknowledgments such as the naming of a library room or building, accompanied by the unveiling of a plaque, honor roll, or similar permanent recognition of the donor's generosity. From the donor's perspective, nothing is more important than this recognition. You must give it to the donor, even if from your perspective the recognition event may seem anticlimactic. Your staff must work with the honoree in a way that satisfies the donor's possible need for ego gratification. Your staff should consult with the donor about the guest list and about other details of the event. When it takes place, you should also have a photographer on hand. You must, in sum, make the event a memorable occasion for the donor. In landing the gift you have achieved an important goal, and now you and your staff will want to work to solidify the relationship with the donor. This is an important element of stewardship.

Fundraising Events

Many people assume that the purpose of a fundraising event is to raise money. However, if the money raised by fundraising events were the only purpose for having them, they usually would not be worth the effort. In fact, many institutions expressly ban such events because they are not cost-effective. It is common for costs associated with even modest fundraising events (modest in terms of the library's outlay) to amount to half or more of the total revenues raised by the event, not including staff time. In all too many ways, and for all too many occasions, the very term "fundraising event" is an oxymoron.

Increasingly, it is imperative to find an underwriter to make more ambitious events financially worthwhile. If you doubt your ability to find someone to underwrite your event costs, you probably should not attempt it. In any case, if your event will probably produce a return of only $10,000 or less, you would be far better off concentrating on one good major-gift prospect than endeavoring to make money by means of a fundraising event.

If fundraising events are not especially reliable or effective in terms of the money they raise, what are they good for? They can, if done properly, enhance your library's image and raise its visibility and prestige enormously. These events can pull into your circle high-powered people who like such events but who would not otherwise be much interested in a library. Putting on chic galas, however, requires a lot of panache on the part of the library director. Here, as elsewhere, the library director must assess her feelings and talents to determine whether she wishes to enter this particular arena.

Beware of one other hazard connected with fundraising events: galas can sometimes introduce preemptive conflict with existing solicitation plans. For example, you might have identified a prospect capable of establishing a $25,000 endowment, but once he has purchased a table at your gala for $2,000, he may think he has made his donation to the library.

Understand the Value of *Content* and *Feeling* in Events

Every event has two elements: content and feeling. Most librarians are accustomed to considering the content of a program. But just as much attention must be paid to the affective elements of a program, to the feelings and emotions that are elicited in the participants.

As the library director, you must keep your eye on two overriding goals. First, people must have fun, and having fun may have more to do with their receiving the right kind of attention than with the actual content of the program. Second, the appropriate statements and ideas must be expressed during the program; it is your job to see that the ceremonial aspects of the occasion are fulfilled.

Some library prospects are interested in the day-to-day realities of library operations; most are not. Most would rather have library matters sketched out to them briefly during introductory or closing remarks at one of your events. The library director and the development team can use the informal portions of an event to develop these points about the library with prospects individually. If you make *your* agenda items for the library the content of your programs, you will bore people. Instead, think of events (and development in general) from the point of view of the prospect, who wants to feel good about the experience of attending the event. Prospects will stop coming to events that do not interest them.

Similarly, you may be interested in controversial political figures or writers who aim to shock their audiences, and you may believe that people who do not share your taste lack sophistication. If you do, fine, but you are well advised to pursue these interests outside the realm of development. Again, always think about your choice of speakers from the point of view of the prospect.

What is it that your events can give potential donors? *Access!* Access to interesting speakers that they would not otherwise hear; access to a stimulating group of attendees; access to a glamorous occasion, such as a black-tie event; access to special places in the library; or, in the case of a Friends-group outing or certain exclusive cultivation events, access to a well-known person's home. (Note: "access" in this context does not refer to borrowing privileges or library services.)

Development professionals frequently refer to making people feel "warm and fuzzy" through events. They recognize that people want to be stirred, moved, and involved in a personal way. These feelings can be evoked by the content of a program or in some other way. People's names might be mentioned publicly; they might involve themselves by asking a question of your speaker; or they might enjoy getting attention from someone important in your library, university, or parent institution, such as yourself or a prominent administrator or faculty member. Be alert to opportunities to give people the kinds of experiences and individualized attention that result in warm feelings about your enterprise.

Understand Your Role in Setting the Tone for Events

Whether the library director knows it or not, his style not only sets the tone for the organization, but establishes its image to the outside world. People around us view things about us in quasi-symbolic terms. Our office, our title, our choice of personal touches, what we choose to reveal about ourselves—all these things are read as symbols by others.[2] To take an obvious example, an orderly office and desk say that things are under control. Messy or cluttered ones convey the opposite message, and that message clings to us whether we know it or not.

We all desire to improve ourselves, and believe in—or at least want to believe in—our abilities to do so. At the same time, we know that there are certain things about our nature that we cannot change and probably should not want to change, so far as doing so might distort our fundamental and integrated personality. Still, our commitment to ourselves carries with it a responsibility to examine how we come across to others.

What if we discover that our image and the symbols that make it up could use some changes? We need not spend long anxious hours poring over *GQ* or *Vogue*, but we might read a book about dressing well; or we might hire someone to advise us about our wardrobe. We can also attend to seemingly small but important details such as, for women, shedding purses or other female baggage before we appear in front of a group, or, for men, being sure to don a coat before appearing in public or at a business meeting.

Everything is symbolic. Rather than getting bogged down in the minutiae of events, focus on the right details, those that can be read as symbols. Think, for example, about what message the choice of a speaker will carry. Be mindful of the appearance of your invitations. Be concerned with the overall elegance of an event.

Think, above all, about how you want to come across, what your performance should accomplish. Be positive and visionary. Remember the story of the two stonecutters working on the reconstruction of St. Paul's Cathedral in London. When asked by Sir Christopher Wren what they were doing, one replied, "I am cutting stone." The other replied, "I am building a cathedral."

Master the Art of Effectiveness in Group Situations

In order to be effective at an event, you must "work the crowd." Working the crowd means taking an active rather than a passive role, and it *is* work. Despite the seeming disingenuousness implied in the phrase, the truth is that people who are good at this do it in a spontaneous and uncalculating way. Operating mostly on instinct, they look for ways of involving people in the occasion and of giving them congenial roles to play. They may, for instance, ask someone to introduce them to someone else or to serve as an official host at a table. They notice those who need attention to be drawn into the spirit of things. *They do not spend time in conversation with their own staff or peers.*

Library directors adept at working the crowd introduce people to others in a way that recognizes and communicates a person's uniqueness (e.g., "Dr. So-and-So is helping us involve book collectors in the library"). When speaking with guests, they know how to listen for random bits of information and deftly link them to the library. They also have a knack for getting people to talk about themselves. They are able to move rapidly from acquaintance to friendship. As a library director, you may face hostile groups all too often. Development offers you a respite from the battlefield. Your prospects will generally be favorably disposed to you and your library; they will want to admire you. Recognize this and enjoy it.

Events are excellent occasions for you to start developing the kinds of skills that will make you a good fundraiser whether or not you are currently a library director. Attend library events and consciously adopt "host behavior" rather than "guest behavior."[3] In other words, make an effort to put others at their ease by greeting them, offering them a refreshment, or making an introduction or small talk. For example, walk up to a stranger, and say, "Hello! I'm so-and-so and I am the head of such-and-such." The person you are addressing will almost invariably respond in kind. From this point it is quite easy to ask another question such as "How long have you been a member of the Friends?" or, "How did you hear about this event?" or, "Are you an alum?" Just keep asking questions, get people to talk about themselves, and they will think that you are charming. Keep the MAGIC formula in mind while you are talking.

As the conversation continues, you can make a powerful point by saying something like, "We do some wonderful things in the library that have an impact on every student and every faculty member at this university. Many people forget this or do not understand it. But you and the other people here today do recognize this and that means a lot to us." If you feel capable of doing so, it is extremely helpful to personalize the library's endeavors by saying something positive about the director's or the president's vision, remembering that almost all donors must believe in the director and his vision before they will make a gift. For example, you might say, gazing respectfully in his direction, "The Dean is such a remarkable leader. Did you know that she [state some amazing fact]?" If they respond, you say something like, "But there is so much still to do to make [the wonderful thing] a reality. That is way we have this [campaign] [program] [you name it] going." That is all you have to do, and then make mental notes of the answers. At some point you might want to thank your interlocutor for coming and express your gratitude for his interest and support. Basically, this is what the development people are doing, too. Ordinarily, they are not equipped with any more information about people than you are, but they may be a little more experienced and comfortable in talking to strangers.

Most people have fears about getting close to others. But you have to take some risks to be a good fundraiser. Fundraising perhaps teaches us to exercise our tolerance and compassion, to shed the tough-guy act that we may have constructed over time. Fundraising requires that we relate to others with empathy. It is this challenge, incidentally, that draws many development professionals to the field.

THE ANATOMY OF A FUNDRAISING EVENT

Since 1988, the library support group at the University of Southern California, the Friends of the USC Libraries, has sponsored a black-tie gala known as the Scripter Award. We include a description of the event because we think it illustrates generally useful ways to think about events and development. This case study is also instructive in three specific ways: (1) it illustrates how a fundraising event can be used to serve a number of development purposes beyond the bounds of the occasion itself; (2) it demonstrates how an idea can be used to connect the library to a glamorous and monied segment of the community; and (3) it provides specific details about how to package and orchestrate an event. Note, however, that the Scripter Award, like any such event, is not without a down side. It has some fairly serious drawbacks, which we have outlined at the end of this case study.

The Scripter Award

The purpose of the Scripter Award is threefold: (1) to raise money for the library's endowment (currently, funds are augmented by a $1 million National Endowment for the Humanities Challenge Grant to the library), (2) to take advantage of the library's special niche by creating a giving opportunity that is attractive to members of the Los Angeles community, and (3) to increase the visibility of the development efforts of the library in several target constituencies.

The Scripter Award is an award honoring "the best realization of a book as a film." The award goes to two people: the author of the book on which a film is based and the screenwriter who adapted the book to the screen. Eligible films—those based on books (of which there are on average 30 a year)—are identified and screenings are arranged for a high-level selection committee, which includes key people in the film industry, writers, and selected members of the board of the Friends. The selection committee also receives complimentary copies of many of the eligible books, which are donated by the film studios and publishers. All voting is done through mail and fax ballots; in this way the committee never has to meet together, allowing it to include busy, prominent people from all over the country.

The first Scripter Award was presented in 1988. The selection committee chose to honor the writers of *84 Charing Cross Road,* a film based on Helene Hanff's story of her transatlantic relationship with an English antiquarian book dealer. Awards were made to Ms. Hanff and to Hugh Whitemore, who wrote the screen adaptation of the book. The film was produced by Mel Brooks and starred his wife, Anne Bancroft, as Ms. Hanff, and Anthony Hopkins as Frank Doel, the shy bookseller. Ms. Hanff was unable to attend the dinner, but Ms. Bancroft accepted the award on the author's behalf. She also presented the award to Mr. Whitemore. Comedian Carl Reiner added a special note to the evening by paying a tribute to the film's producer, Mel Brooks.

In 1989, the award went to Anne Tyler for her novel *The Accidental Tourist* and to Lawrence Kasdan and Frank Galati, who cowrote the screenplay. The reclusive Anne Tyler, who rarely makes public appearances, sent her husband, writer Taghi Modarressi, to accept the award on her behalf. Mr. Kasdan and Mr. Galati were in attendance, and Geena Davis, who later won an Oscar for her performance in the film, presented them with their awards.

In 1990, the recipient of the Scripter was *Awakenings,* Oliver Sacks' book describing the experience of patients who had long suffered from sleeping sickness and who were awakened by the controversial drug L-dopa. Robin Williams, who played the character in the film based on Dr. Sacks, presented the Scripter Award to him. Dr. Sacks, in turn, presented the screenwriting Scripter Award to Steven Zaillian for his adaptation of *Awakenings.*

In 1991, the Scripter Award went to *Fried Green Tomatoes* by Fannie Flagg, who adapted her book to a screenplay with help from Carol Sobieski. Ms. Flagg, who began her career as a comedienne and had a cameo appearance in the film, was the star of the evening. She was joined by actresses Dixie Carter, Diane Ladd, and, via video, Kathy Bates.

The Scripter gala itself is planned with the kind of care that might be associated with a televised award ceremony. In general, there is a great effort to provide guests with as much entertainment value as possible. Apart from acceptance speeches, which of course cannot be controlled, everything else is planned, timed, and scripted in advance. Film clips are shown at various strategic points during the evening, and music and lighting are used to heighten effects. The master of ceremonies for all of the Scripter Awards to date has been long-time Friends' board member Hal Kanter, an Emmy-winning comedy writer.

The Scripter Award was the idea of two members of the Friends board, and this made its success a possibility from the beginning; the Friends not only took immediate ownership of the award but recognized how they were uniquely poised, through already established ties to Hollywood, to make it take off. They recognized how the award capitalized on the university's geographic location and its focus on film studies. They also saw how this award would enable the library to build a bridge between itself, representing books and authors of books, and Hollywood, representing films and screenwriters. While it is true that all these factors and links are unique to the USC library, it is equally true that other settings have their unique assets, too. The challenge is to find your own imaginative ways to connect your library with those unique assets.

In a relatively short time, the Scripter Award has become a sought-after writing honor in the film industry. Film studios, distributors, agents, and others connected with films based on books see the Scripter Award— which is presented in January or February, just weeks before the voting process for the Academy Awards comes to a close—as a timely way to increase the visibility and legitimacy of a film.

Staffing and Organizing the Event

When the event was established, the development staff of the library, who reported to the Dean/University Librarian, included a development officer who was in charge of the Friends, other annual-giving programs, and middle-range endowment gifts. The staff also included a full-time events coordinator who reported to the development officer. In addition, there was a major-gifts development officer who was working on a capital campaign to build a new library and who reported to the central development office of the university. The University Librarian assigned the responsibility for the Scripter Award to the development officer in charge of the Friends.

The development officer, working with the Friends' board and under the ambitious leadership of the University Librarian, organized the event and selection committees. The event committee sold individual tickets and tables and worked with the library staff on various aspects of the preparations for the event, though, in actuality, the library staff did virtually all of the work as far as the preparations were concerned.

Publicity

Through a contact on the Friends board, an outside public-relations firm that was willing to give the library a significant discount was hired to handle a full-scale publicity campaign. By the third year, the ongoing selection process of the award recipients was covered by the "trades"—*The Hollywood Reporter, Variety,* and *Premiere*—on a regular basis. Articles about the award dinner appeared in the *Los Angeles Times* as well as in the local papers. These articles mentioned and usually carried photos of the socially prominent people who attended the event. By the third year, the dinner was covered by *Entertainment Tonight* and by a number of television news programs.

Obviously, the publicity was valuable to the library and its development efforts, especially because, in busy and news-saturated Los Angeles, it is very difficult to obtain press coverage. The publicity was also important to the success and effectiveness of the award itself. Through publicity, the award gained legitimacy. Finally, the award has been successful in part because it filled a niche of its own. It beamed a spotlight where it seldom shines in Hollywood: on writers. This is perhaps the major reason why the award has so quickly become an important one to the film community.

Creating an Identity

The initial task for those involved in the Scripter Award was to give it an identity. First, the venue was an important consideration. In order to keep the library the focus of the Scripter Award dinner, organizers felt that it was essential to hold the event in the library rather than in a hotel or even in another location on campus. They chose the grand reference room in the main library because it had the right feel and look and was large enough to accommodate almost 300 people. The logistics of converting the room to a banquet hall with a minimum disruption of service were considerable. (Because the event necessitates the closure of the main reference department for about a day, some students and staff members opposed the event on principle.)

Once a venue had been established, the development staff hired an outside professional designer to create a look for the award that entailed designing an elegant logo and a graphic theme, which were then used for stationery, invitations, and the menu/program for the event. The logo was also used on a grand scale by a lighting specialist who projected it onto the wall in the entry area the evening of the event. A caterer, considered by many to be the best in Los Angeles, was engaged to prepare the dinner with an emphasis on elegance. The caterer incorporated the logo into the dessert, which was a *livre en chocolat* featuring the Scripter logo "S" on its cover. In general, many imaginative and subtle touches of this type were designed into the event to reinforce themes and linkages.

Advancing the Development Effort

The development staff has used the Scripter Award in a number of ways to advance the fundraising efforts of the library. First, there was, of course, the goal to raise funds through the event itself. Each year, the staff worked to secure underwriters for the event since it is very difficult to realize a sufficient return on ticket sales alone, despite the fact that these monies are augmented by advertising sold in the event program. In 1992, individual seats were priced at $250, and tables of twelve were priced at $2,500, $5,000, and $10,000 depending on how well-placed they were in the room. The constant expansion of the Scripter invitation list, now numbering 2,500 names, is an ongoing goal of the development staff. (Incidentally, a special software program prints addresses on envelopes from the mailing list data base in a style that resembles calligraphy; machine-produced mailing labels would not be appropriate for an event of this type.)

Presenting awards to prominent people is one of the oldest tricks in the fundraising book. Often this device is used to raise support from the award winner's associates. The Scripter Award, however, functions a little differently. Though it involves prominent people, Scripter's support comes from a broad donor base that is independent of the award recipient and that includes the USC community and the various contacts of the Friends. And though the studio that produced the film usually is interested in supporting the event (as are agents, distributors, and others associated with the project), Scripter is not used to "hit up" the award winners themselves or their associates for support.

In addition to the income realized by the event itself, the Scripter Award serves a development function by providing excellent cultivation opportunities for donors and prospects of all kinds. The event committee, for example, encourages the sorts of interaction that socially prominent people engage in—and all of these interactions are in this case focused on the library. The selection committee provides a mechanism for cultivating prestigious people who are drawn by the chance to select an award recipient; in the process, they acquire ownership of the event and become prospects. Underwriters receive recognition at a level that positions them for even higher levels of giving. They are extensively thanked for their generosity on the evening of the gala before a large and prominent audience, their names are emblazoned on the programs, and they sit at the head table and are accorded royal treatment. For such donors, underwriting events like the Scripter Award is the best giving opportunity they could imagine.

The Scripter event is also an excellent entry-level giving opportunity for people who normally would not be interested in the Friends or in the library. For these people, an event like Scripter might be the only thing that would entice them into the library. Once they are inside, however, many discover it to be a much more interesting place, with much more interesting people, than they had ever imagined.

The Scripter fundraiser helps the Friends and its board focus on development matters—especially on building the endowment—in a way that is exciting to them. It also increases the board members' own giving, since it is generally understood that they are expected to purchase a table themselves.

Another way the development staff uses the event is as a tie-in to development organizations on campus, especially the USC Associates, the university's premiere support group. Professional fundraisers involved with such groups are always looking for occasions they can use as cultivation events for their prospects. In this way, the Scripter event promotes goodwill among colleagues and raises the visibility of the library among both fundraising professionals and volunteers on campus. Moreover, it sometimes results in gifts later on from people who attended the event.

However . . . There Are Drawbacks

If the Scripter Award illustrates some of the advantages of a fundraising event, it also demonstrates most of the problems. It is a great deal of work, especially for the amount of money it raises, on average, $50,000 per event. The Scripter event does not just take a couple of months of intense effort before the event, but effort all the time (momentum must be sustained, screenings arranged, underwriters sought, mailing lists updated, etc.). In addition, it may distract some prospects away from other, higher-priority giving opportunities in the library (for example, we were in the midst of a top-priority building campaign during the Scripter Award's first three years). It also may introduce competition with other established university fundraising events (in our case, for example, with development efforts in the Cinema School). And, as we noted earlier, the event is not popular with some of the students and many of the librarians. Some people from both groups oppose part of the library being closed for a day while the event is set up. Indeed, at the first Scripter event, which was held on a Thursday night, a small contingent of students protested outside the library as guests arrived for dinner. In subsequent years, the negative impact of the event on students was mostly eliminated by scheduling the event on Saturday night when the library was closed.

Still, the lesson could be drawn from this, and from a multitude of other experiences, that if the impact of such events and their fit within the library's niche are not carefully considered, they may effectively become the fundraising equivalent of a black hole.

What Is *Your* Hollywood?

The Scripter Award's strength is that it taps into Hollywood, a glamorous and monied segment of the community, to the benefit of the library. Every library is in a community that has some special quality which sets it apart, and many communities have vibrant sectors where the action and money are. Finding and tapping that aspect of your community is an important key to successful fundraising. What is *your* Hollywood?

NOTES

1. We do not include book sales as an event category since the revenues they generate usually do not reach a level that qualify them as serious development activities. In most cases, publicizing them as such would send a damaging message about the scale and vision of the development program.

2. See Robert B. Cialdini, *Influence: How and Why People Agree to Things* (New York: Quill, 1984), pp. 215–223.

3. Susan RoAne. *How to Work a Room: A Guide to Successfully Managing the Mingling* (New York: Shapolsky Publishers, Inc., 1988), pp. 27–29.

8 Making It Personal
<u>Demystifying Fundraising from
Foundations, Corporations, and
Planned-Giving Prospects</u>

This chapter introduces the rudiments of raising money from corporations and foundations, and from planned giving prospects. The chapter aims to provide you with enough information to direct these aspects of your fundraising program without overwhelming you with needlessly detailed data. Our remarks are primarily addressed to the university setting, though many of the principles discussed are generalizable to other library settings.

Today, in central development offices of universities, there are fundraisers who specialize in corporations and foundations, and there are other fundraisers who specialize in planned giving. Together, these areas involve certain technical complexities for the professional fundraiser. However, for the library director, the basic issues they raise and the basic approaches they require differ little from those described previously in connection with raising funds from individuals.

In all three of these areas of development, the most effective way to begin raising funds is to cultivate relationships with the specialists in your university so that the library benefits from their expertise and contacts. These relationships should be ongoing, and you should maintain them in the way that you would a relationship with a colleague whose professional goodwill you have come to rely on. That this goodwill is necessary becomes apparent when you consider that, of all the voluntary support going to higher education in 1990, less than 1 percent was designated to libraries.[1] It is important for librarians to stay visible and pursue relationships with central development staff so that the library is not forgotten in favor of more traditional, high-profile areas.

PUBLIC VS. PRIVATE FUNDS

In general, government dollars are the hardest to raise. The applications for government grants usually require enormous amounts of work, and the awards are often relatively small. Relative to its financial yield, the securing of government money receives a disproportionate amount of attention from librarians, both in practice and in the library development literature. Perhaps this is so because librarians feel comfortable with government grant applications which, in comparison to face-to-face fundraising, seem to be relatively clear-cut processes.

As a result, librarians tend to be knowledgeable about and good at grant applications. When they need help they can find it both in the literature and from the agency to which they are applying. Since the purpose of this book is to provide guidance on those aspects of library fundraising that have not previously been addressed, we do not specifically address government grant applications. We assume that your library will, as a matter of course, be engaged in pursuing such grants, and we wish you success. However, your librarians should handle the application processes, or you should engage a grant writer on a consulting basis. Coordinate these activities with your development staff, but do not assign them to it. *Government grants are not where the money is.* Individuals are your best prospects.

FOUNDATIONS AND CORPORATIONS AS GIVING ORGANIZATIONS

The key to unlocking giving from foundations and corporations is contained in this simple statement: *the same principles that apply to raising money from individuals apply to raising money from foundations and corporations.*

All of us regularly read about large foundation or corporate gifts to libraries, and we think, "I want one too!" With vexation and a touch of envy, we find ourselves asking, "Why aren't we doing something about approaching this or that organization?" The answer is that foundation and corporate gifts are not the "open-to-all-comers, all-it-takes-is-a-good-proposal" affairs we sometimes imagine them to be.

In fact, large corporate and foundation gifts often are the result of a process that is almost identical to the one for individual givers and rarely the result of an impersonal grant-application process. Behind every large foundation or corporation gift to a library is a unique story. These stories almost invariably involve individuals who, as heads of corporations or foundations, have become committed to a library exactly in the manner that individual prospects do, but with the added dynamic of their organizational affiliations. And these stories have implications for you as a unique institution: just as it is not realistic for you to consider approaching individuals who are committed to other institutions, so it is not realistic for you to hope to duplicate another library's success story in terms of its foundation or corporate gifts.

But it is possible to create your own success story by keeping the following points in mind.

1. *Individuals—not corporations and foundations—are your best prospects.* Relative to overall giving in this country, corporate and foundation gifts account for a small percentage of the philanthropic pie, roughly 10 percent annually.[2] We have pointed out that your energies should be focused on your best prospects, and that these are individuals. Do not forget this if and when you decide to launch out in search of corporate and foundation support. That said, corporations and foundations tend to be supportive of education and educational institutions. Indeed, corporate and foundation giving amounted to 42 percent of all voluntary support for higher education in 1989 and in 1990.[3] But, of the voluntary support for current operations designated to academic libraries in 1990, about 50 percent came from individuals, about 40 percent came from foundations, and only 10 percent came from corporations.[4]

In some libraries, support from foundations and corporations may exceed these percentages, but when this happens it is because individuals with access to foundation or corporation money become committed to the library's cause.

2. *Identify and cultivate key individuals within corporations and foundations.* The most effective strategy is to identify individuals within important foundations and corporations who have some tie to your institution and, having done this, to cultivate them. In essence, you need a friend at court. A good relationship with such a friend will allow you to build a partnership with his organization. Once you have a partnership, you can then work together with people in the organization to develop a successful proposal. Just as with individual prospects, you build incremental commitment by sharing drafts of the proposal. By the time the final proposal is submitted, you should have a clear idea of the likelihood of your success.

Unfortunately, many people adopt a strategy of identifying *possibly* sympathetic foundations or corporations rather than *already* sympathetic individuals, and of proceeding from there. Generally, this strategy works only when, at some stage in the process, you also identify a volunteer who knows someone at the particular organization and who can intercede on your behalf. The worst way to go about raising money from foundations and corporations is simply to read about them and send them proposals out of the blue with no champion to back them within the organization.

3. *Work with the central development office.* One of the most productive things you can do if you want to bring in corporate and foundation dollars is to cultivate the central development staff responsible for this area in your university. Build relationships with them. If they understand

and adopt your goals and if they like and respect you personally, they will work on your behalf. They will know, for example, which volunteers have ties to which foundations and companies. They will have well-established relationships within various organizations and will be creative in coming up with ideas and approaches. If they do not like you, however, they will not be helpful. As one central development staffer in foundation and corporation gifts remarked, "they will simply ignore you."

Foundations

In light of the previous discussion, it should be no surprise that some of the largest foundation gifts going to libraries today are being awarded without any formal applications or proposals. In these cases, individual trustees feel a deep personal commitment to a library and serve as its advocate within the foundation. This is not to deny that foundation funds can be secured through formal channels, especially small- to medium-sized gifts, but the fact remains that your most promising potential funders are those foundations to which your organization has a tie in the form of a relationship with an individual.

Nevertheless, every library wants to go to Pew, Mellon, Kresge, Keck, and the other big national foundations. Every library hopes that it can, by filling out an application, land a grant from these philanthropic heavyweights. Such ambitions will likely meet, however, with some formidable obstacles. Assuming you do not have a contact within any of these foundations, you will have several additional challenges beyond the fact of going in cold. For one thing, it may be difficult to get clearance from within your own organization to make the approach. For another thing, it may be difficult to establish relationships within the ranks of program officers and directors of big foundations because they tend to have heavy work loads and a high rate of turnover. Finally, many foundations will consider only the institution's highest funding priority, and all too often this is something other than the library.

Corporations

There are two levels of corporate giving: a level of large corporate grants and partnerships and a lower level at which, in some companies and firms, managers above a certain rank are given an allocation for charity that they may dispense as they wish. People with access to these latter funds can be excellent candidates for upper-level Friends memberships or purchasers of tables at your gala. However, they are not sources of large corporate gifts.

Some libraries have tried to attract corporate gifts through the formation of corporate Friends groups. Such programs entail considerable planning and marketing, but they have not met with much success. This is not surprising: as we mentioned, corporate giving accounts for a mere 10 percent of all giving to academic libraries; and earlier we pointed out that just a few major gifts will account for 90 percent of total giving. Hence, using an annual-fund approach to reach corporate sponsors is to marry the least successful fundraising approach for libraries with the least responsive target group.

Fee-based services are another method that some libraries have begun to use with the idea of raising money. However, as of this writing, most of them are barely breaking even, let alone turning a profit. And those that are making money are only producing very modest amounts of income.[5]

A much more productive approach to corporate fundraising is to look for opportunities for creative partnerships. Corporate gifts, it is well known, reflect a kind of enlightened self-interest on the part of a company. Rarely do companies give away money simply to be altruistic. Usually they are generous because there is something in it for them. To be successful in this arena, you must be prepared to think in terms of forming partnerships—of making mutually satisfying, yet ethical, business deals.

What are some examples of creative deal making? These might include working with a major furniture manufacturer to develop new workstations, working with a major publisher to develop and test electronic publishing, or working with a major computer company to design library applications. Such partnerships often result in in-kind gifts from corporations. Outright cash gifts usually come about only after these business-like partnerships have been successfully forged.

PLANNED GIVING

Planned, or deferred, giving is a broad term encompassing a variety of financial arrangements in which a donor gives an asset, such as stocks, real estate, books, manuscripts, photographs, or some other appreciated asset, to a nonprofit organization or institution, but still reaps benefits from the gift as long as she lives. In essence, the institution agrees to assume the burden of investing or managing the asset, while the donor enjoys a tax break and receives regular payments from the recipient organization. The following are some general recommendations with respect to planned giving.

1. *Cultivate relationships with the planned giving development people in your university* just as you would with the corporate and foundation people. Cooperative relations with the planned giving office can result in big gifts to the library. Many times planned giving donors approach the university without fixed ideas about where their gift should go; the planned giving professional is in a prime position to guide that decision. Since this area is highly technical, the advanced discussions of a

planned gift are now handled mostly by specialists, many with legal or tax backgrounds. When you get to this point with a prospect, such specialists will help you with the details and logistics of the gift.

The planned giving office also will help you with efforts to identify planned giving prospects. For example, they may arrange luncheons or seminars on estate planning or they may sponsor similar events in order to present the concept of planned gifts to people who have been identified as prospects for gifts of this type. Your development officer will see that the people you have identified as planned giving prospects are invited to these events. If you can persuade the planned giving people to present the library as an attractive giving opportunity at these gatherings, they can be excellent agents for directing planned giving candidates to the library.

To impress the planned giving people with your own seriousness, it might be well to offer to host one of these events in the library. You should also try to involve the planned giving staff in discussions of your prospects. Finally, read the brochures of the planned giving office, which usually are not technical and can give you an overview, from the prospect's point of view, of what that office can accomplish.

2. *Learn how to recognize a prospect who might benefit from a planned gift.* The ideal planned giving prospect has no heirs, is in his or her late sixties or early seventies, and has been involved in your organization in some way. Also, a married couple in the same age group with no heirs can be good planned giving prospects. People without heirs naturally think of leaving their assets to a nonprofit organization. People with heirs also think about their estates, and sometimes consider making gifts to nonprofit institutions; but they tend, out of ignorance, not to realize that if they leave their estate entirely to heirs it will be taxed so heavily that their deaths will primarily benefit the government.

The maxim "charity begins at home" may be relevant in more ways than one to your efforts to benefit from planned giving. Many people in your own university and in your own library will fit the profile of the ideal planned giving candidate. Faculty and emeriti faculty, for instance, understand the value and importance of the library. Moreover, it is common, unfortunately, for faculty members to harbor grievances against their departments and thus come to see the library as their campus "home." Emeriti faculty members sometimes require extra attention and patience, but some of them have amassed surprising wealth, and many of them have valuable collections of art and books. Even scholars of modest means frequently own property. In some parts of the country, real estate values have skyrocketed to such an extent that the gift of any property will translate into a major gift.

Your university may be able to provide you with a list of retired professors (and, perhaps, those about to retire). Review the list with people in the administration who know the faculty and work with the planned giving experts on your campus to contact, cultivate, and solicit them. Analogous approaches can be considered with regard to members of your own staff. For obvious reasons, however, pursuing such gifts may be problematic, and we advise discretion if you elect to do so.

3. *Keep planned giving in front of your supporters.* Whenever possible—at events, in newsletters, and in brochures—encourage your audience to think of the library when they think about estate planning. Obviously, this must be done with sensitivity and tact. Because they are nonthreatening, newsletters are good vehicles for describing planned gifts. Another good technique is to involve, perhaps on your Friends' board, attorneys and accountants who can work with their clients to direct planned gifts to your library.

Because they require so much work in advance, planned gifts tend to be unusually well-considered. For this reason, they tend to be given to institutions to which the giver feels a strong tie. Unfortunately, it is the rare university alumnus who thinks about the library when considering a gift to his alma mater. Usually, donors think first of the school or program they attended. For this reason, the library should be as visible as possible among the planned giving staff and before prospects. It also helps if the library is an institutional priority.

4. *Understand the motivations behind a planned gift.* One of the major motivations behind establishing trusts is the avoidance of estate taxes. Estate taxes are a concern these days for a surprisingly large number of people, being, as they are at present, levied on net assets of more than $600,000 for an individual and $1.2 million for a married couple. The equity in a house, plus other assets, such as stocks or a business, often exceed these amounts. In addition, many people have taken advantage of tax-deferred employee savings plans. Thanks to the effect of compounding interest in those savings plans, the accumulation of assets by the American public is growing dramatically.[6]

Two Types of Deferred Gifts

There are many different types of planned or deferred gifts, so many, in fact, that you will want to work with planned giving professionals whenever the possibility of a gift arises. Therefore, rather than offer a technical description of planned giving vehicles, this section describes a simple model for thinking about types of planned gifts.

One of the most common is the *charitable remainder trust.* Charitable remainder trusts may be structured in several ways, but they basically involve the donor's giving an asset and receiving regular payments equaling a certain percentage of the value of the asset. Another type of planned gift, less popular now, is the *charitable lead trust,* in which an institution receives the income from the donor's asset for an agreed-upon period, after which the asset is transferred to the donor's heirs. Both arrangements can reduce gift and estate taxes and provide a charitable deduction for the donor.

The following tree-and-fruit analogy helps clarify the difference between these two deferred-giving instruments.

Charitable remainder trust = The donor gives the tree and keeps the fruit.

Charitable lead trust = The donor gives the fruit and keeps the tree.

Even though the charitable lead trust is not used much now, the fruit-and-tree analogy can be a useful tool for explaining the basics of a planned gift to a prospect.

The Planned Giving Call

When you initially broach the idea of a planned gift with someone, you say something like this: "Planned giving allows you to change the situation (you delicately avoid saying 'of your death' at this point) from one of involuntary taxation, where the bulk of your assets goes to Uncle Sam, to one of voluntary giving, where the bulk can go to the library." And then you can use the tree-and-fruit analogy to give the person a rough idea of how a planned gift works. While talking with the person, try to find out as much as possible about his personal situation, and then suggest, if appropriate, that you introduce her to "an expert from the Development Office."

You will probably accompany the expert on the first call. This call should be handled much as you would handle any other development call. There are, however, two important but very sensitive pieces of information you need to know about planned giving prospects: their overall wealth and their age. The planned giving officer will probably lead into the discussion by raising the question of the prospect's goals. Do they want to leave something to their children? Do they need income now? Would they like to give you their property but retain a place to live for their lifetime? Because the value of a person's estate is critical in terms of taxation (in 1991, $1.2 million for a couple results in a 43 percent tax; $600,000 for a single person results in a 37 percent tax; and a $2.5 million estate gets taxed at 55 percent), your colleague will be trying to get a sense of the person's net worth. "What do you own?" is one way of putting the question. The prospect's age is also very important information because the IRS will determine tax deductions on the basis of life expectancy. Asking people their age directly can sometimes be difficult. One technique for dealing with this is to suggest a range ("Are you over 65?") or to ask when they were born.

At this early stage, you will keep things very simple during the giving-information part of the meeting. You will explain how you can help the prospect accomplish his goals, you will promote your institution and your cause, and lastly you will lay the groundwork for a later visit. After this first call, you can probably turn things over to the planned giving officer, who will continue to nurture discussion. When things have progressed sufficiently, the planned giving officer will suggest a meeting with the prospect's attorney or accountant to begin to draw up an agreement.

Appreciated Assets

A donation of appreciated assets can produce a double tax benefit for the donor when the contribution is structured so that the appreciated value of the assets escapes taxation. For example, Mr. and Mrs. Donor own securities worth $100,000 that they purchased for $20,000. (Assume they are in the 35 percent tax bracket; 28 percent federal and 7 percent state.)

The Wrong Way to Do It

If the securities are sold, the $80,000 of appreciation will result in a capital gains tax of 35 percent: $28,000. The net proceeds of $72,000 ($100,000 less $28,000), if contributed, would save taxes of $25,200 ($72,000 × 35 percent). The end result is that the Donors would pay tax of $2,800 ($28,000 less $25,200, or, if you prefer, 35 percent of the $8,000 differential between $80,000 and $72,000) and the nonprofit organization would receive $72,000.

The Right Way to Do It

A better way to structure the gift would be for the Donors to give the appreciated securities to the organization outright. The capital gains, in this case, would not be taxed. The full fair-market value of the gift would be allowed as a charitable deduction. The Donors would also get a charitable deduction of $35,000 ($100,000 × 35 percent) when they filed their next tax return. The end result is a double tax savings, in which the Donors would avoid capital gains taxes of $28,000 on the $80,000 of appreciation and would get a $35,000 tax break because of the charitable deduction, for a total tax savings of $63,000. In addition, the library would receive the full $100,000.

This example also applies to other kinds of assets, such as real estate, antiques, and other items of value. It is possible to treat a collection of books, manuscripts, photographs, or other library materials as an appreciated asset. These items receive a full fair-market-value deduction if their use is related to the purposes of the university. This is good to know because often (especially in special collections) older people will come to you asking you to buy their collections. The valuable ones frequently carry price tags that make them out of the question as far as a purchase is concerned. In these cases, a planned gift can provide a win-win outcome for both the collectors and library.

How Much Should I Emphasize Planned Giving?

Though planned giving prospects are abundant in and around universities, planned gifts themselves are not as abundant as the prospect pool might suggest. There are several reasons for this. From the point of view of the prospect, planned gifts can seem complicated; they seem too complicated for most people after about age 75. Another drawback from prospects' perspectives is that planned gifts sometimes involve more talking and more effort than wills, with the result that the prospects spend more time on the uncomfortable subject of their demise.

There are also some impediments from the development side. Most planned gifts take a huge amount of effort. It is not unusual for such a gift to require 18–24 months and 13–18 visits. Generally, the only planned gifts that go fast are the ones that come from people who are financially sophisticated and already understand the benefits that can be realized by this type of gift, especially through the avoidance of capital gains taxes.

Some planned giving professionals will tell you that the biggest gifts are made in people's wills, and that you should spend at least as much time encouraging this form of giving as you do the more complicated kinds of planned gifts. As it is undeniably true that many of your biggest gifts will be testamentary, you should emphasize this form of giving as much as discretion and good taste allow.

The best advice is to not overemphasize planned giving in your program, but to know a viable planned giving prospect when you see one. Above all, remember that planned giving and fundraising from corporations and foundations all reflect the uniqueness of your situation. The types of gifts that come to your organization will reflect its own unique support base.

NOTES

1. Council for Aid to Education, *Voluntary Support of Education* 1990–91, 2 vols. (New York: Council for Aid to Education, 1991), vol. 1: *National Estimates and Survey Summary*, p. 14.

2. American Association of Fund-Raising Council (AAFRC) Trust for Philanthropy, *Giving USA: The Annual Report on Philanthropy for the Year 1989* (New York: American Association of Fund-Raising Council, 1990), p. 6.

3. Council for Aid to Education, p. 2.

4. Ibid., p. 14.

5. Julie L. Nicklin, "Many Institutions Conduct Research for Companies for a Fee, but Others Assail the Practice," *The Chronicle of Higher Education,* 38 no. 24 (February 19, 1992): A29–A30.

6. James Flanigan, "Malcolm Forbes' Lesson on Estate Taxes," *Los Angeles Times* (March 4, 1990): sec. D, p. 1.

9 Enhancing Your Image

Communicating Strategically about Your Library

This chapter is not about development per se but about something larger: your library's image. Image involves not only public relations but the broader notion of *communicating strategically* to those people who are interested in your library—be they donors, patrons, or members of the public. This chapter takes a brief excursus into the new field of strategic communications, describing techniques that can dramatically enhance your effectiveness in a variety of situations.

With the continuing globalization of communications in the 1980s, CEOs of major companies and other high-profile figures around the world found that they could no longer simply manage their companies but, much like American political candidates, they also needed to be concerned about their constituencies' attitudes and behaviors. When they sought help they found it not only on Madison Avenue, as they had in the past, but also in the skills of political consultants. The business of strategic communications consulting was born. Strategic communications is an amalgam of techniques used to affect public opinion: market research, management consulting, advertising, public relations, and indirect lobbying. The field is a broadening of what had been earlier referred to as "spin-doctoring."

This chapter draws lessons from strategic communications management and applies them to libraries. While many traditional spin-doctoring techniques are manipulative, and therefore at odds with the basic philosophy of this book, many valuable insights may be gained from the field of strategic communications. And, after all, we are not applying these techniques for the benefit of a politician, a corporate raider, or a South American dictator, but we are promoting valuable collections, marketing useful services, and raising money for a worthwhile cause. This chapter will explain how you can be more effective by managing your communications strategically. For our purposes, we will define strategic communications management as an effort to affect, through the use of appropriate communication instruments, the image a constituency has of your library.

After an initial discussion of the difference between development and public relations, this chapter provides an overview of some of the basics of strategic communications for libraries: how to understand who your important constituencies are and what and how they think about your library, and how to use the five major communication instruments to tell your story. The chapter concludes with a discussion of image. Our goal is not to instruct you on the techniques of public relations—writing press releases, pitching stories, placing advertising, printing brochures, and the like—but to help you know how to *think strategically* about your library's communications.

PUBLIC RELATIONS AND DEVELOPMENT

Though both public relations and development serve to advance your library, they are very different in their focus on constituencies, their use of communication instruments, and their ultimate goals. For this reason, a discussion of their differences is a good way to begin to illustrate the concepts of strategic communications.

Public Relations	Development
• Promotes good image	• Raises money
• Seeks a wide and diverse audience	• Focuses on donors
• Uses mass media	• Uses personal contact
• Goal is awareness	• Goal is giving

If you confuse public relations with development, you risk having expectations for your development program that do not match your activities. In some cases this results in development officers performing nondevelopment functions such as writing annual reports, editing newsletters, drafting press releases about new services, and lobbying the public-relations office for placement in the alumni magazine of articles about, for instance, the on-line catalog. Increasing the amount of publicity your library receives and producing promotional materials are not development; they are aspects of public relations. Some libraries have even tried to market salable merchandise, like note cards, as a fundraising activity. Merchandising may raise the public's awareness of your institution, but in most libraries it rarely brings in more than small change since the costs of production and distribution are likely to negate revenues from sales.

Yet, because public relations and development have the common goal of advancing the library, an effective public-relations effort will complement the development program and vice versa. If you can afford it, hire your own public-relations person for the library. If that is not possible and you are in a university, you can assign your development officer to work with the individual in the central public-relations office who has the library as his beat. If your library is in a nonuniversity setting, consider contracting with a private public-relations firm. Whatever you do, be careful not to burden your development officer with too much responsibility for publicity. Instead, activate the right people in your organization to make your public-relations effort effective.

STRATEGIC COMMUNICATIONS

The essence of strategic communications for libraries is to use the right tool (communication instrument) for the right job (communicating a message to a constituency). Librarians make decisions about their communications every day when, for example, they choose to place advertising in the newspaper for community programs or publish resource guides for their patrons. A clearer understanding of strategic communications can allow librarians to become sophisticated about image building and issue management.

Strategic communications goes beyond the vague notion of "raising visibility," a goal mentioned often in organizations but one that, because it is not strategic, usually results in a diffuse message. For example, many Friends-of-the-Library newsletters are filled with stories about services and staff, though they are meant to interest donors and other friends outside of the library. Another example involves the newsletters that some reference departments in university libraries publish for faculty. Such an instrument is usually ineffective because faculty members' needs are so specific that only by initiating personal contact will the librarian ever understand or meet those needs. (This is why the invisible college—interpersonal communication among academic colleagues—is alive and well.) Both of these cases are examples of communicating *un*strategically.

Constituencies

A large and disparate number of people know about your library and have an opinion about it. This group is made up of a number of identifiable subgroups or constituencies. For a university library, these might include: students and their parents, faculty and staff, the university administration, friends and alumni, foundations and corporations, off-campus library users, other libraries and universities, and members of the general public.

Each of these groups has an image of your library, an image that may be defined as the sum of feelings, beliefs, attitudes, impressions, thoughts, perceptions, ideas, recollections, conclusions, or mind-sets that the constituency entertains about your institution.[1] By paying careful attention to how you and your library communicate to your various constituencies, you can positively affect your library's image, an effect that will benefit all areas of your library including your development efforts.

Think about your various constituencies and which are important to you in various contexts. Which are most important to your development program? Which to your public services program? Which should you, as a director, be spending the most time on? It is critical that you focus the right messages on the right constituency. Students have little money and are already paying for their education—they are not a concern of your development program unless their parents are prospects for your library. Messages about the details of your library's services are most important to the constituencies who use your library regularly, not to those who do not use it, like many of your donors. However, messages about the *quality* of your services may be very important to donors, even if they do not use the library regularly.

The Five Communication Instruments

There are five major communication instruments that you can use to communicate with your constituencies: advertising, publicity, personal contact, atmospherics, and outreach materials.[2]

Advertising

Since you pay for it, you can carefully control advertising. Advertising is especially useful when you want to communicate a sensitive, complicated, or timely message that is not, however, related to a hot news story and that in consequence might not otherwise receive public attention. For the most part, advertising is a straightforward and well-understood communication instrument, although it is interesting to note that, more and more, it is common to see advertising disguised as publicity.

Publicity

Publicity is information controlled by the medium that is communicating it, usually newspapers, magazines, television, or radio. Whether it is initiated by the institution through a press release or a story verbally "pitched" to a reporter, publicity cannot be tightly controlled. The advantage of publicity is that it carries more weight with the public than a paid message since it takes on the legitimacy of its medium and of the media system as a whole. In addition, publicity is free (apart, perhaps, from staff time spent on press releases, phone calls to pitch a story, and interviews).

Publicity—even seemingly good publicity—is not always good for your institution. For example, sometimes librarians will seek publicity in order to "raise the visibility" of a program or collection that is threatened for fiscal reasons. Their strategy is to try to protect the program or collection by attracting media attention. This approach can backfire, especially if the case for support has not been built over time, and, rather than make a program seem indispensable, it can increase doubts about its necessity in the minds of the very people in a position to axe it. In such a case, a carefully targeted communication strategy using personal contact and outreach materials would have better results.

Personal Contact

Though the least far-reaching method of communication, personal contact is the most powerful. This is why, even in a media age, politicians still spend time shaking hands. (It is also why we so strongly recommend personal contact in development situations.) The extent to which you can affect how your staff interacts with others on a daily basis will perhaps make the biggest impact on your library's image. It also means that, as a director, the amount of time you spend meeting with people and the people with whom you choose to meet are among the most important decisions you make each day.

Atmospherics

Atmospherics are those qualities of your physical plant that have an effect, whether conscious or subliminal, on visitors. A powerful, positive message is communicated by your library if obvious attention is paid to its design and aesthetics in addition to its pragmatics. A powerfully negative message is communicated all too often in libraries when form is sacrificed to function, resulting in a sterile, cold environment. Think of how the President uses the Oval Office as a prop when he wants to communicate an important message. *Your office,* and other spaces in your library, can be used similarly if they are suitable.

Outreach Materials

Outreach materials are, of course, printed or audiovisual materials that communicate information to targeted audiences. Your outreach materials, both development-related and otherwise, are a communication channel through which you can make a big impact. Your outreach material can set the tone, style, and image for all of your library's communications. Be sure you have style guidelines for in-house publications. Assign more formal publications for external use to your public-relations person who should produce them in collaboration with a professional designer who, in turn, will give your publications an identifiable "look."

Outreach materials, being the communication instrument of preference for librarians, merit detailed consideration in this chapter, especially where development publications are concerned. As we have said, personal contact is almost always the best communication instrument for use with prospective donors. Professional fundraisers often repeat this adage: people do not give money to brochures, they give money to people. Still, there are times when brochures are appropriate and useful. Sometimes your donors will tell you that the need exists for a brochure. Sometimes you will discover that you need to package and describe a program in order to help volunteers and prospects understand it. But you do not need publications just because others have them, and as we noted earlier, you certainly do not need a case statement.

Though people do not give money to them, development brochures can serve several useful functions. First, they get people's attention. They send a message that says you are serious about the program being described in the piece and that the program is a priority for your organization. Second, brochures serve as reference guides and can be used by a donor as a point of reference after the program has been discussed orally with her. They are also useful for spelling out any complicated aspects of the program. Third, a publication gives the program a reality and tangibility and thus makes the program more legitimate and official in the reader's mind. You might, for example, want to establish a mechanism for encouraging people to make donations in honor or memory of someone. If your volunteers have expressed an interest in making these kinds of gifts, and if you have other reasons to believe that such a program would be successful, you might want to package the program in a brochure. The brochure would describe the program, highlight the recognition that the donor would be given, and provide a reply mechanism. Simply suggesting to your volunteers that they should consider making small memorial gifts is not likely to be as effective as having a program fully described in a printed piece.

Brochures and other written materials are never substitutes for face-to-face meetings. A development brochure that describes a high-level gift opportunity, such as a named endowment program, is not a direct-sales piece and would not be successful as a mass mailing. Though it should be accompanied by a person-to-person discussion, neither is such a brochure a "talk piece" for use during a development call; it is not there to guide you or the donor through a solicitation. Its value in the development process is as a follow-up to an oral presentation.

Most people do not read brochures, they skim them. The design of the brochure will make more of an impact than its text, so pay close attention to a brochure's graphic and visual design. In order to have quality publications, you should consider hiring an outside professional designer since few libraries have access to outstanding graphic arts talent in-house. Amazingly, many of the country's top libraries ask librarians untrained in publication design to design their publications; even worse, when choosing areas on which to economize they will elect to cut costs on publications. Brochures are a very visible means of presenting your library to the public, and you do not want the presentation spoiled by amateurishness or cheapness.

There are a few points to remember in working with a designer. First, do not let your designer lose sight of the purpose of your piece. You must know exactly what you are trying to accomplish with a brochure so that your message is not lost. Sometimes, for example, a designer will encourage you to use quotes set off from a text block because these allow him to break up attractively a page or a panel. He will not be concerned that quotes might not suit the particular brochure. Other times a designer may want to create something avant-garde in style. However tempting this approach may be, you must remember the importance of warmth, and remember, too, that to most people libraries represent tradition and the safeguarding of the past. An avant-garde style may not be appropriate. In general, you will find in working with a designer that the careful thought you have given to your purposes and uniqueness will begin to pay off as you attempt to express them visually.

Sophisticated Uses of Strategic Communications

A sophisticated understanding of strategic communications will benefit your library in innumerable ways and will certainly be helpful to the development program. Politicians, as we all know, use every available communication instrument to get their messages across to voters, sometimes in very sophisticated ways. You can do this, too. If it helps, think of yourself as being in a race for political approval with your library as your platform. The following examples show how, by thinking strategically about your communications and by matching the right messages, constituencies, and communication instruments, you can manage your communications.

A common problem for academic libraries is that they have poor reputations with their students, despite their best efforts to be responsive and accommodating. The library's hours are not long enough, its books are not shelved fast enough, it does not have the books they want, and it does not have enough seats. The students regularly revile the library in their newspaper, occasionally picket the library, and petition for increased hours and services, refusing to believe that the library can neither afford the expense nor justify it in terms of actual use.

In this case it is clearly not necessary to do a lot of research on what the constituency thinks. The important point to recognize is that some students, who may even be a minority, are controlling the discourse. Naturally, you must be sure that you are doing everything you can to address legitimate complaints. But often this is not enough. You must also change the nature of the discourse.

While your first impulse may be to respond directly to the accusations by means of a letter to the editor, consider instead an altogether different strategy. Try enlarging the discourse to include positives. One good way to begin is to identify some positive responses to the library on the part of students. Examples might include the senior class making a gift to the library, a survey that finds a high level of satisfaction in library services overall, growth in endowment or acquisitions budgets, or a student who values the library, has used it in a unique and effective way, and is willing to go on record to say so.

With just one or two positive elements, you could construct a mini-campaign to alter the prevailing perception of your library. You could take out ads in the student newspaper thanking the senior class or describing the survey results, and you could write stories for various campus publications. It would also be important to talk about these developments with known policy- and opinion-makers. Be creative. You could print a proclamation about the senior class gift that could be read by the library director at your black-tie gala, after which a member of the senior class could present a check to the university president. With a little effort, there is no limit to the imaginative ways you can get a new message about the library before your various constituencies.

ENHANCING YOUR IMAGE

Earlier we defined image as the sum of feelings, beliefs, attitudes, impressions, thoughts, perceptions, ideas, recollections, conclusions, or mind-sets that a constituency entertains about your institution. Now we are ready to examine in more depth what your library's image is and what you would like it to be.

Everything about your institution "talks": signs, stationery, business cards, documents, the way phones are answered, the way employees dress, newsletters, logos, how patrons are helped, facilities and grounds, vehicles, exhibits, displays, brochures, invitations, announcements, bulletin boards, and publications. All these send messages about your library, both overt and tacit, to those who come into contact with them and therefore contribute to its overall image. If you coordinate these things and attend to their quality, your library's image will be attractive and focused; an uncoordinated approach will result in an image that is unappealing and confused.

The best way to understand your library's image is to talk with members of your various constituencies. There are formal devices that you can employ to do this—focus groups, interviews, and surveys—or you can simply have informal discussions with people and make notes.

You may find that others' perceptions of your institution bear little relation to its actual condition. Sometimes peoples' perceptions of an institution do not keep up with the institution's changes. This phenomenon is sometimes appropriately called "image lag."[3] For example, though your administration may be engaged in several pioneering initiatives, the administration preceding yours may have had low visibility, so that people may not know about your new endeavors or even imagine that there might be any.

However you go about researching your image, remember the principle of limited information gathering. Chances are you already know a great deal about what your image is and what you would like to change about it. Your research need not be any more extensive than filling in a few blind spots you might have in your understanding of the strengths and weaknesses of your public image. One of the reasons you know so much about your image is that you, too, are a member of a number of your library's constituencies. You may be a staff member, a faculty member, a regular user, or even a donor. If you are honest with yourself in the process, you can make a number of observations about your library's image using simple techniques such as the image audit and the image self-test described below.

Audit Your Image

What is your library saying to its constituencies? One way to answer this question is to perform an image audit. You can begin by collecting examples of all of your library's publications and laying them out on a table. Ask yourself how they look together. Are they coordinated? What image do they project? Do they say, "Quality," or do they say, "Aw, shucks, we can't spend time or money on this"? You can examine signage and other tangible factors in a similar way. Mark a day on your calendar devoted to image and spend it walking around your library, looking and listening carefully to what it is communicating, and thinking and strategizing about ways to improve it.

Take the Image Self-Test

In addition to conducting an image audit, take the following image self-test.[4] Rate your library from a low of 1 to a high of 10 on each question and total your ratings for all 10 questions to find your score.

1. We take care of our facilities (e.g., library buildings, furnishings, signage) because we know that they say a great deal about who we are and the pride we take in what we do.

   1   2   3   4   5   6   7   8   9   10

2. The library is represented in community affairs and events because we believe it is an intellectual and cultural center of the community and we are its representatives.

   1   2   3   4   5   6   7   8   9   10

3. Our signage is professional, effective, and attractive.

   1   2   3   4   5   6   7   8   9   10

4. There is a detectable air of vigor in our library.

   1   2   3   4   5   6   7   8   9   10

5. Telephone courtesies and first-impression training are part of our employee orientation programs.

   1   2   3   4   5   6   7   8   9   10

6. Employees are evaluated on their interpersonal skills as they relate to the public; they have time to "be nice."

   1   2   3   4   5   6   7   8   9   10

7. We do what we can to arrange our services in a comprehensible way.

   1   2   3   4   5   6   7   8   9   10

8. When it comes to publications, we care not only about content and accuracy, but about appearance, too.

   1   2   3   4   5   6   7   8   9   10

9. Promoting the collection is in some ways as important as the money spent on building it.

   1   2   3   4   5   6   7   8   9   10

10. We regularly examine our public image and take steps to enhance it.

   1   2   3   4   5   6   7   8   9   10

Score

10 – 30	Your library is definitely talking behind your back, and it is not saying nice things.
40 – 70	Your library's image, while not abysmal, could use some attention.
80 – 100	Good work. Your library's image is a credit to the hard work you and your staff do.

This survey is meant to encourage you to think through the issues underlying each question. A low score may indicate serious problems in your organization that you will do well to correct. Knowing what you know now, you can take a sophisticated, multipronged approach to changing it.

In the decades ahead, it will be more important than ever to affect attitudes and behaviors by communicating strategically. Thinking about the messages you are currently transmitting, and making intelligent choices about the communication instruments you employ, will enhance your image and benefit not only your development programs but your public relations as a whole. You can be your own spin-doctor.

NOTES

1. For this definition of image, we acknowledge Robert S. Topor, *Institutional Image: How to Define, Improve, Market It* (Washington, D.C.: Council for Advancement and Support of Education, 1986), p. 1.

2. Robert S. Topor, *Marketing Higher Education: A Practical Guide* (Washington, D.C.: Council for Advancement and Support of Education, 1983), p. 88.

3. Topor, *Institutional Image*, p. 2.

4. Adapted from Robert S. Topor, *Your Personal Guide to Marketing a Nonprofit Organization* (Washington, D.C.: Council for Advancement and Support of Education, 1988), pp. 138–139.

10 Thoughts on the Future of Library Development

Only connect!
E. M. FORSTER

These days it seems that discussions about the rapid changes taking place in libraries dominate our field's literature, conferences, and our daily working lives. The expanding technological environment demands that librarians be attuned to change, ready to anticipate it, and able to respond adroitly. As a result, our focus has shifted from the internal functions of libraries to external technologies, markets, and opportunities. As we anticipate change, we become more outward looking and future oriented.

This shift in orientation bodes well for library development. An outward focus and an openness to change and to nontraditional approaches are complementary to fundraising. We have begun to connect, to seek new kinds of relationships, to forge partnerships, to be entrepreneurial. In this way, change has helped librarians to create an environment that is alive with opportunity.

But precisely how the changes we anticipate for our libraries will affect the way we raise funds in the future is another question. For example, what happens if the library, though still the *intellectual* center of learning, is no longer the *geographical* center, so that people have less reason to visit libraries in the future, relying instead on data bases and networks?[1] Or what will be the impact of a library leadership that increasingly is made up of people from the computing field? The purpose of this chapter is to discuss generally how such issues might affect the fundraising climate of the future.

For instance, as library functions become less visible and increasingly electronic, we may hunger for the tangible and the traditional. Ironically, special collections may become more "special" than ever before. As these collections gain in value, so do the librarians who manage them. They are the keepers of objects for which electronic substitutes will not do, and these librarians are invaluable assets for library leaders of the future. Their knowledge and skills can be fostered to benefit the development of the entire library.

As technology-oriented individuals come into leadership positions, a tendency to want to make development "scientific" may arise. However, library leaders who believe they can create a development agenda in the same way they can create a technology agenda risk oversimplifying and dehumanizing their development efforts. Successful development will always depend, utterly and absolutely, on careful management of individual relationships. Whatever the future holds, one thing is certain: unless we stay in tune with our donors and our organizational environment, we will never know how to make the connections that will bring success in raising funds.

Keeping things personal will most certainly be the overarching challenge of development in the future. For this reason, direct mail and telemarketing are areas of fundraising that will probably diminish in importance. Rote or mechanical fundraising methods, that is, will probably be less effective in the future. Though direct mail would seem to be a natural for the socially-concerned-but-overly-busy members of our society, it is stirring concerns about its wastefulness and environmental impact. Though the ability of direct-mail marketers to more accurately target probable givers continues to improve, mail approaches can only go so far. Nor does the future look bright for telemarketing. Legislation is limiting telephone solicitations and, in any case, telephone technology is capable of screening calls.

As nonprofit organizations become more active and sophisticated in their fundraising, "compassion fatigue" may reach epidemic proportions. We are already feeling weary and overwhelmed by the many causes competing for our attention. How can we prioritize our giving when we receive appeals from so many worthy organizations? In many instances, the appeals touch similar areas of concern. Should we give to the Wilderness Society or the Sierra Club? Should we give to organizations devoted to saving the rain forests or to preventing erosion of the ozone layer? In the field of education, this quandary is especially difficult. There are so many aspects of education at so many levels that even the informed layperson may find it difficult to evaluate the claims of each.

On the positive side, overall giving in our country may very well increase. Baby boomers are already giving more as a group than the older age groups, which have traditionally been the most generous givers. Baby boomers, of course, attended colleges and universities and used libraries in unprecedented numbers. There is every reason to hope that a significant degree of their charity will be directed to education and to libraries.

However, in one area the baby boomers will not be as beneficial to charities as was their parents' generation: they will not have time to be volunteers. This is especially true of women, who have entered the work force to an extent almost inconceivable to their mothers. The effect this will have on organized fundraising will be significant. One effect may be that more of the work of raising money will be done by the directors of nonprofit organizations and their development officers.

Some librarians say "we are people of the book, not of the checkbook," as if to suggest a fundamental incompatibility between librarianship and fundraising. To subscribe to this view is to miss a crucial truth about fundraising. Fundraising is not simply about the checkbook; it is about communication. And what is our business, after all, but *communicating about information?* Fundraising provides a powerful vehicle for taking messages about the book—and the many other important things we are about—to others.

The day is gone when librarians were librarians and fundraisers were fundraisers. The very definition of what it means to be a library leader has changed to include fundraising as an essential function. If librarians want to have a role in shaping the future of libraries, they will have to engage in fundraising.

The librarians who will be most successful at raising money will be those whose vision, leadership abilities, and personal qualities will enable them to communicate the special qualities and merits of their libraries. Understanding your unique setting is crucial to your success now; it will become even more important in the future.

Learning to be a good fundraiser takes effort. Every fundraiser learns through trial and error. In this book, we have tried to present the fruits of our experience, observations, and thought. We hope these, plus your own good instincts and intuition, will give you a start.

If, as librarians, we can become adept fundraisers, we can ensure the future excellence of libraries. One of the best reasons for having a development program is that it allows *us* to articulate the direction of, and set the priorities for, our libraries and to take this message to others. If we want to succeed, we must pursue our vision for the future of libraries, and we must connect with those who will help us to realize it.

NOTE

1. For example, see the issues raised by Peter Lyman in "The Library of the (Not-So-Distant) Future," *Change* (Jan./Feb. 1991): pp. 34–41.

Recommended Reading

Bennis, Warren, and Burt Nanus. *Leaders: The Strategies of Taking Charge.* New York: Harper & Row, 1985.

Cialdini, Robert B. *Influence: How and Why People Agree to Things.* New York: Quill, 1984.

_____. "What Leads to Yes: Applying the Psychology of Influence to Fund Raising, Alumni Relations, and PR." *CASE Currents* (January 1987): 48–51.

Kelly, Kathleen S. *Fund Raising and Public Relations: A Critical Analysis.* Hillsdale, N.J.: Lawrence Erlbaum, 1991.

Leavitt, Harold J. *Corporate Pathfinders.* New York: Viking Penguin, 1986.

Miller, Robert B., and Stephen E. Heiman. *Conceptual Selling.* New York: Warner Books, 1987.

Nadler, Gerald, and Shozo Hibino. *Breakthrough Thinking: Why We Must Change the Way We Solve Problems and the Seven Principles to Achieve This.* Rocklin, Calif.: Prima Publications & Communications, 1990. (Available through St. Martins Press, New York, 212–674–5151.)

Tannen, Deborah. *You Just Don't Understand: Women and Men in Conversation.* New York: William Morrow and Company, 1990.

Topor, Robert S. *Institutional Image: How to Define, Improve, Market It.* Washington, D.C.: Council for Advancement and Support of Education, 1986.

_____. *Marketing Higher Education.* Washington, D.C.: Council for Advancement and Support of Education, 1983.

Index

Victoria Steele is one of the few librarians in the country who has also been a professional library fundraiser. Her M.L.S. is from the University of California, Los Angeles (UCLA), where she also headed two special collections before becoming Director of Development for the UCLA Libraries and the Graduate School of Library and Information Science. In 1988, she became head of the Department of Special Collections in the University of Southern California (USC) Libraries. At USC, she takes an active role in fundraising for the libraries. She also has been active in a variety of professional organizations, particularly the American Library Association.

Stephen D. Elder is a Senior Development Officer at the University of Redlands. During the writing of this book, he was a Development Officer for the University of Southern California (USC) Libraries. He has a B.A. in Journalism from the University of Utah and has worked as a news reporter, editor, and marketing manager. He earned his M.A. in Communications Management from the Annenberg School of Communications at USC, where he studied the design of public communication campaigns. He has a wide range of public relations, marketing, and development experience in the nonprofit setting.